THE
KATAS

THE
KATAS

The Meaning behind the Movements

KENJI TOKITSU

Translated by Jack Cain

Inner Traditions
Rochester, Vermont • Toronto, Canada

Inner Traditions
One Park Street
Rochester, Vermont 05767
www.InnerTraditions.com

Library of Congress Cataloging-in-Publication Data

Tokitsu, Kenji, 1947–
  [Katas. English]
  The katas : the meaning behind the movements / Kenji Tokitsu ; translated by
Jack Cain.
      p. cm.
  "Originally published in French under the title: Les Katas: Arts martiaux &
transformations sociales au Japon by Éditions DésIris, Paris"—T.p. verso.
  Includes bibliographical references and index.
  ISBN 978-1-59477-348-8 (pbk.)
  1. Martial arts—Social aspects—Japan. 2. Martial arts—Japan—History. I.
Title.
  GV1100.77.A2T6513 2010
  796.80952—dc22

                                                                    2010015217

Printed and bound in the United States by Lake Book Manufacturing

10 9 8 7 6 5 4 3 2 1

Text design by Jon Desautels and layout by Priscilla Baker
This book was typeset in Garamond Premier Pro with Centaur and Eurostile used
as display typefaces

CONTENTS

PART FOUR
Persistence and Transformation
in a Traditional Culture

PREFACE

This book arose out of the inner struggle in me between the world of *katas* and the process of my settling down in France.

I was born in Japan and lived in my native country until I was twenty-three. By then, I had already practiced martial arts for ten years and had been introduced to kata as an essential component of martial arts teaching.

Kata includes a strict framework that defines what you seek and sets boundaries on your inner and outer world, and in so doing, it defines your position in relation to others. In my case, moving to France disturbed this framework. How I saw my relations with others was brought into question.

For example, on the level of language, it was unthinkable for me to address someone older in a familiar way, and the French language gave me no way to show the respect that can be shown in Japanese. From a broader point of view, the equality in relationships in France seemed to oppose the Japanese longing for a hierarchical society.

I later found correspondingly in all the traditional Japanese arts some aspects of kata as I practiced it for twenty years in *karate*—where the word *kata* has a precise meaning. In pondering the meaning of *kata* as the basic set of moves in the practice of an art, I began to discover the mental structure and the particular kind of identifications* that overlaid each practice. The definition of *kata* that I had come to from this preliminary study turned out to be the most obvious expression of a social reality that was much broader and much harder to grasp.

In Japanese the word *kata* has two principal meanings written with two ideograms:

1. "form" 形 etymology: "outline of an exact representation using brush strokes"
2. "mold" 型 etymology: "original form made from earth." For a long time, this ideogram has also meant "tracks or traces left behind," "ideal form," "law," "custom."

The word *kata* then stands for two things: First, it means the image of an ideal form and its exact outline as it is going to be represented. Second, it began to be used to designate the codification and transmission of knowledge based on a prescribed set of technical movements with the body, but we don't know during which era this meaning arose. This historical aspect is, in fact, quite significant.

Indeed, kata developed out of a long Japanese tradition and must be looked at within its historical context. The basic stages of Japanese history help to explain aspects of the concept of kata as well as shedding light on facts and recent modes of behavior that would otherwise not be understandable or would even be considered crazy.

Having arisen within the dominant social class—the warrior class—kata is still present today in many fields, even though the Japanese themselves may be unaware of it. Other cultural factors have become attached to kata, resulting, over the centuries, in a structure that underlies many of Japan's various characteristics.

Through the lens of my own search for a personal identity, in this

---

*[The author uses the word *identification* throughout the text in the sense of "associate oneself inseparably with." Identification is a key concept among the ideas he is conveying. —*Trans.*]

text I endeavor to explain the role and the importance of kata in Japan and why it still concerns the Japanese, caught as they are between what is clearly a stable tradition and the rapid changes that are taking place in their social structure.

In this regard, the case of Yamaoka Tesshu, a nineteenth-century warrior, illustrates perfectly the idealized image of a man. This image is still present in contemporary Japanese society. His life, entirely dominated by the attainment of kata and entirely focused on perfection, conveys a way of being and a manner of thought that cannot be dissociated from Japan's social context.

PART ONE

An Introduction
to Katas

1

TESSHU,

OR A MODEL LIFE

Katsu Kaishu tells us:

> July 19, 1888, was a terribly hot day. When I arrived at my friend
> Yamaoka Tesshu's place, I was greeted by his son Naoki.
>
> "How is your father doing?" I inquired.
>
> "He says that he will die soon."
>
> There were numerous visitors in the home, and Tesshu, dressed
> in a white Buddhist robe, was calmly seated among them in *zazen*
> meditation posture.
>
> Addressing myself to him, I said, "Have you come to end of your
> time, *sensei*?"*
>
> He opened his eyes gently, smiled at me, and replied without
> appearing to be in pain.
>
> "Thanks for having come, my dear friend. I am close to leaving
> for the state of Nirvana."
>
> "May you graciously attain the state of Buddhahood,"† I said to

---

*In its literal meaning, *sensei* means "he who was born before me." This term is used
for someone worthy of respect, for example, someone further up in the hierarchy, or a
teacher. It is also used in everyday discourse simply to convey a certain degree of respect.
†The expression *jō-butsu* in Japanese means, "to reach the state of Nirvana" as attained
by the Buddha. For someone who is Japanese, the expression is also used to say "one
has died well."

him as I stepped away. That very day, taken by the stomach cancer that had been eating away at him for several months, Tesshu succumbed without leaving the meditation posture in which his body remained even after death. Two days before, he had said to his son, "I am suffering an unusual pain today and would like to see my friends before I die."

While Naoki was taking care of these final wishes, Tesshu bathed, dressed himself in a clean, white kimono* and assumed a zazen posture.[1]

As an adolescent I was bowled over by this tale. A death like this seemed to me to be the reverse of an intensity of living, and it was linked to a question that is inevitable at such a young age: "How do I live my life?" Later, as I read more about Yamaoka Tesshu, I understood just how symbolic this ideal image of life and death was for the Japanese. The persona of Tesshu became stronger, more vivid, because his death showed none of the serenity of an old man who fades away gently but rather the departure of a man scoured by disease who stands up to his suffering—a total self-mastery and the continuation, up to the last moment, of a hard-won art of living that had been guided by precise cultural forms.

This story is more than a simple anecdote; there is a sociological aspect to this example of Tesshu's death. It occurred at the pivotal period in Japan when the feudal era was ending and the Meiji era was beginning—officially, 1868.

Yamaoka Tesshu's life was devoted to the way of the sword, enhanced by the practice of Zen. He was born in 1836 to the Ono family, a wealthy family of warriors (*bushi* or *samurai*), and he was given the name Ono Tetsutaro, although he is better known by the name he assumed: Yamaoka Tesshu. Thanks to the family fortune, his father was able to arrange the best possible education for his warrior-class son, and Tetsutaro took to it with great eagerness.

---

*In Japan, the clothing in which the dead are buried.

While he pursued his study of the philosophical texts of Buddhism, Confucianism, and Shintoism, which constituted the basic education of the time, he began, from the age of nine, to engage in the practices of swordsmanship, calligraphy, and Zen. Even though he was living in the provinces, he had access to eminent teachers in each of these disciplines.

Notably, Inoue Hachiro, a very highly regarded teacher of swordsmanship, came from Edo.* Twelve years old at the time, Tetsutaro, armed with a wooden sword, found himself assigned a daily exercise of ten thousand *tsuki*.† This was followed by training with an opponent. Inoue pitilessly struck and goaded his student's body. Even though he was wearing padded exercise armor, Tetsutaro would often pass out when thrown against a wooden wall.

Thanks to this arduous training and to his unshakable will, Tetsutaro made remarkable progress. At fourteen, he received a master's certificate in calligraphy, and even today, a good number of his calligraphic works survive.

At seventeen, he went to Edo and entered Master Chiba's swordsmanship school, one of the three most important schools in the city, where his teacher Inoue himself had trained. Master Chiba Shusaku, sixty-nine at the time, was the founder of this school. The main courses were taught by his son Eijiro. Two thousand students attended the two-story school, which had a large training room (*dōjō*) on the main floor and dormitory space for about fifty disciples on the floor above.

Many swordsmanship practitioners who had been trained in these great schools went on later to join political movements and took part in the wars of restoration (Meiji Ishin). This was the period in Japan's history when, because the sword had regained a real social function, the intensity of the training was extreme. Among the many adherents, a few reached the pinnacle of this art.

---

*The former name of Tokyo.

†A *tsuki* consists of striking with the point of the blade while holding the sword with both hands. Done properly, all the body's strength, as well as the force behind breathing, must accompany each move.

Tetsutaro, who had already trained with Inoue for years, made further progress by training even more vigorously than before. He obtained his graduation certificate in swordsmanship at the age of nineteen and garnered a reputation for strength as witnessed by his nickname Oni Tetsu (Tetsutaro, "demon strength"). The effectiveness and force of his tsuki were well known throughout the school.

In 1854, at eighteen, Tetsutaro entered the National Martial Institute (Kobusho). Also in this year, an American fleet appeared for the second time in Japanese waters to demand the opening of Japan's commercial markets, which had been closed for two and a half centuries. At the same time, a complex transformation was beginning within Japanese society. At the institute were taught all the traditional martial arts—as well as the recent addition of naval studies arising from the external threat represented by the arrival of the American fleet.

In following the way of martial arts, Tetsutaro was seeking what might be called "a permanent state of existence." In Japanese culture, this expression designates a state in which words are no longer of any use—existence has completely merged into art, leaving no place for the word.

He was barely twenty when Master Chiba Shusaku said to him, "Tetsutaro, I could train you, if you like."

The training consisted of combat exercises with a bamboo sword and protective attire. Tetsutaro thought, as did the other disciples, "Even though he's a grand master, he's more than sixty and his strength must have declined. His son Eijiro, the young master, has to be stronger than him. Maybe I have a chance of beating him." So Tetsutaro replied to Chiba, "Yes, master. I would be honored."

They took up their swords. At the sight of the master's face behind his helmet, Tetsutaro cringed in spite of himself.

"Go ahead when you like," the master said.

But it was impossible. Surrounding the master's body, Tetsutaro felt the emanation of a powerful energy (*ki* or *kiai*) that completely prevented him from moving. Tetsutaro, "demon strength," remained frozen, sweating profusely. About thirty years later he confessed to his own students, "I was like a frog captured by a snake." The real adept (*meijin*) is truly at an extraordinary level.

Shortly afterward, Chiba Shusaku died at the age of sixty-two, but from this day onward, Tetsutaro's training intensified even further. During this period his javelin teacher, Yamaoka Seizan, who was also his best friend, drowned. This event led to a problem of inheritance for the Yamaoka family. Within the patriarchal system of the warrior class, the choice of a successor was essential to the continuation of the family name. Because Seizan left no heirs, only his fifteen-year-old sister Fusako remained.

Considering the strong bond that existed between Tetsutaro and the Yamaoka family, the younger brother of Seizan, Takahashi Kenzaburo (adopted by the Takahashi family, therefore the Takahashi heir), proposed that Tetsutaro marry Fusako. In spite of the relative poverty of the Yamaoka family and the wealth of the Ono family, and in spite of the disparity in their respective social levels, the marriage took place. At the age of twenty, Tetsutaro became the heir of the Yamaoka family—the family of his best friend and, in a way, his predecessor in the way of martial arts.

He began to work at the National Martial Institute as an official instructor along with many adepts from the most famous schools. At the same time, he continued to attend Master Chiba's school. In this way, he was brought into contact with people of many different political persuasions.

During this period, which was later called Baku-matsu (the end of the shogunate), two major political currents appeared within the warrior class: one of these, Dabaku, strove to reinforce the shogunate system, while the other, Kinno, strove to establish a new system of government in which the emperor would, as before, wield power.

The governments that the warrior class had formed always respected the supremacy of the emperor, but he remained outside the political arena, serving a purely symbolic role as head of state. When Tokugawa

Ieyasu founded the shogunate system in Edo in 1603, even then he had to respect protocol and have himself named Sei-i-Tai-Shogun (Great General, Vanquisher of Enemy Barbarians) by the emperor, who then found himself relegated to his palace, where he lived and was respected but was bereft of power.

The title of grand shogun had been created at the end of the eighth century to refer to the earlier duties of a warrior, Sakanoue-To-Tamuramaro, whom the emperor Kammu sent to the north of Japan to crush a barbarian revolt (Ezo).

During this period, imperial power was in full ascendancy, and the role of the warrior class was being delineated. Yet by the time Minamoto Yoritomo took the title of grand shogun in founding the first warrior-class government (1192), the original meaning of the title had disappeared. The grand shogun then became simply the warrior who was accorded supreme political power.

The warrior era in Japan lasted from 1192 until 1868, and during this time, warriors participated in the government. The successive leaders took the title and privileges of sei-i-tai-shogun, which was usually abbreviated to shogun. Even though he had been stripped of all power, the emperor alone could bestow this title and legitimize the executive, thereby reactivating the ancestral forms from which the ritual derived its force.

Tetsutaro lived at the end of the Edo period, a time when the power of the warrior-class government was in sharp decline and the country was facing threats from abroad. During this period of decline of the shogunate, bringing the imperial system into question would have shaken the whole Japanese worldview. Also, the ideologues that opposed feudalism sought support in redoubling the emperor's power: originally, legitimacy went back to the emperor from whom the founder of the shogunate had received his title and his power. One group therefore advocated stripping the shogun of his power in order to restore to the emperor his original role.

Faced with the threat of colonization, which was felt acutely after so many had witnessed what had happened in China, the shogun had nothing to propose except to maintain the current system—that is, a very elaborate and rigid hierarchical structure that oversaw an agricultural society with little technical development and an archaic military system.

The advocates of a reorganization of the country to ward off external forces clashed violently with the conservative tendencies maintained by the shogunate. During the Tokugawa shogunate, Japan experienced two and a half centuries of feudal peace by cutting itself off almost completely from the outside world (Sakoku). As a weapon of war, the sword had become a symbol, and its practice had become, for the warriors, an affirmation of their position at the top of the hierarchy. It turned out that the political and ideological clashes between the two trends that divided the warrior class took the form of sword fights. So the sword enjoyed once again a full revival—which was followed in the end by sword fighting's symbolic and actual disappearance.

At the National Martial Institute, Tetsutaro was in constant contact with these divergent trends, but the revolutionary ideology did not suit him. As a trustworthy man, he continued to be faithful to the shogun, and at the same time, he demonstrated a deep loyalty to the emperor. For him, one did not bring the other into question as it did for other warriors for whom loyalty to the emperor had become synonymous with opposition to the shogun. For Tetsutaro, the way of the sword was so much a movement inward that he remained, for the time being, outside the political movement.

In 1863, at the National Martial Institute, when Tetsutaro was twenty-seven, he met Asari Matashichiro, a great adept who was fifty-nine. Tetsutaro wanted to challenge him in training combat so that he could gauge his own progress.

At the dōjō everyone was astonished at Tetsutaro's nerve, because following the death of Chiba Shusaku, Master Asari was considered to be the most eminent swordsman of his time.

Asari took up a bamboo sword (*shinai*) and said to Tetsutaro, "Go ahead."

Declaring himself very honored for the lesson, Tetsutaro placed himself before Asari. But as soon as Asari took up his on-guard position, Tetsutaro stifled a cry of astonishment. The master had raised his sword over his head, holding it with both hands and remaining perfectly motionless. Tetsutaro could find no chink in his posture—not in Asari's chest, not in the stomach—even though Asari was mostly exposed. He had felt the same sensation eight years before, as he faced his now-deceased master, Chiba. Asari's refined body seemed like a rock and radiated an irresistible force. This energy literally blocked Tetsutaro.

Nevertheless, gathering all his energy, Tetsutaro lunged, putting his whole body behind the tip of his sword. Immediately, he received a sharp, violent blow on his head and his vision clouded. Trying to pull back on his sword, which had pierced nothing but thin air, he received a second blow to his head. If it had been other than bamboo, the sword would have sliced his head in two.

As he stumbled home, only one thing remained in his head—Asari's sword. Three days later, still haunted by this vision, he returned to the school, driven by the following thoughts: "As long as I have not conquered Asari's sword, my sword is dead. . . . As a true adept, Asari has flexibility on the outside and strength on the inside. His awareness breathes, knowing the fineness of combat, understanding his adversary's vulnerable moment even before the adversary has made his attack. . . . My life now has only one aim: to conquer his sword."

To reach Asari's level meant, however, that Tetsutaro had to develop his mind with Zen. Asari's sword haunted him: "Since that day, I never stopped training, but I was unable to find any way of beating him. Nevertheless, from that day on, I did combat training during the day and meditation in the evening in order to discover combat breathing. When I closed my eyes and thought of Master Asari, he rose up before my sword like a mountain, and I could find no way out. This must be because of my innate inability and my lack of sincerity."

Tetsutaro often slept in his master's dōjō with his bamboo sword still in his hands, because, once the evening training was finished, he would continue on his own, and sometimes he would fall asleep deep in thought. Asari would strike him as he slept. Without the slightest astonishment, he would assume his stance. He was ready at every moment.

Even though he had assumed the goal of surpassing his master's level, Tetsutaro, a shogun *bushi* (samurai), was jostled by events. In January 1868, the advocates of the shogun suffered a decisive defeat, perpetrated by the combined forces of the southern feudal clans who favored the restoration of imperial power and were continuing their unstoppable advance toward Edo, where the shogun had taken refuge.

For the feudal power of the shogunate, two possibilities emerged for the shogun: conduct a decisive battle around Edo, or yield to imperial power in order to avoid a useless bloodbath and fratricidal battles.

Considering the threat of invasion by the Americans, the English, the French, and the Russians, the shogun decided to choose the second path, judging it necessary to preserve the fighting strength of a country that was going to have to unite or perish. In August 1868, imperial power was thus restored, and the Japanese state was established in European fashion around the Meiji emperor.

Even though he was a vassal of the shogun, Tetsutaro had played an important role in the reconciliation of the two parties and was approached to assume an important position in the new state. In 1872, he was named chamberlain and educator of the young emperor, who was then twenty years old. This same year, at the age of thirty-seven, he assumed the name of Tesshu.

And this was how Tesshu made his way through this period of social upheaval, bearing in himself the essential values—in the true sense of the word—of the warrior. For him, the point of convergence of these values was two-fold: in society, the emperor for life; and in our inner world, the sword. These two aspects made up for him the *bushidō*,* the warrior's way, significantly different from *budō*, the way of martial arts. The reach of bushidō was greater because of its cosmogonical aspect and the multiple values that it espoused. In fact, it is an amalgam of Buddhism, Confucianism, Shintoism, and martial arts, with, as its core value, respect for the feudal lord, followed by respect for the emperor.

At the beginning of the restoration period, the bushidō-educated warrior class played a pivotal role in the rapid modernization of Japanese society. In fact, this role demanded a significant investment in the service of the emperor and, from that time forward, the expansion of imperial power through the conquest of Western technology. It was based on the principle that the warriors supplied the greatest number of officials within the new Japanese state.

This evolution had the effect of increasing the production power of a capitalist Japan that was beginning to test its wings, and at the same time, it created antimony between this social movement and the traditional values on which it was based. The influence of the dominant ideology of bushidō on the other classes contributed to the training of generations of ardent workers by, for example, honoring each person's contribution and hard work and his loyalty to his superior.

Within this whirlwind of social change, Tesshu was far from forgetting Master Asari—his master and adversary. In addition to his work for the emperor, Tesshu continued to train with the sword and to practice meditation in his personal dōjō, called Shumpukan (House of the Springtime Breeze), surrounded by his numerous disciples. Master Asari had withdrawn from teaching since the restoration of the imperial regime, but Tesshu always had the master's image in mind, and one

---

*Nitobe Inazo wrote in *Bushidō* (Philadelphia: Leeds and Biddle, 1900) that he had received his own moral education not from religion, as is the case in the West, but from bushidō. According to this author, up to the end of the nineteenth and until the beginning of the twentieth century, bushidō provided moral education for the Japanese. Even though it's not clear that bushidō could be considered an educational factor for all social strata of these times, for the warrior class, bushidō remained the educational equivalent of moral and religious education for Westerners.

day, his Zen master said to him, "Even though your eyes are clear, you put on dark glasses. That is why you do not see the real moon."

In 1877, his Zen master gave him a *kōan** on which Tesshu meditated for a long time. Meditation is confined not to the time we are seated in meditation; instead, it must penetrate into day-to-day life and effect a qualitative change.

On March 30, 1880, when he awakened, Tesshu was enlightened and attained *satori.*† As often happened in his dream, he took his sword and faced his master, but this time, Asari's sword, which had always rebuffed him like a huge rock, had disappeared. Tesshu got up immediately and called his foremost disciple who lived in the house, "Koteda! Koteda! Come right away! Get your armor and fight me!"

They stood face to face. Immediately, Koteda put down his sword and bowed, his hands on the floor, saying, "I am lost, master. I cannot continue."

Koteda later related, "I had been receiving my master's training for a long time, but I had never perceived such a strange intensity—nothing that powerful—as that which radiated from my master's sword on that day."

Tesshu requested an interview with master Asari right away and challenged him to combat for the first time in seventeen years. They took up their positions. Asari looked at him for a moment and then lowered his sword, saying with great emotion, "Finally, you have arrived. You have acquired the essence and the intelligence of the sword. I congratulate you. . . ."

In saying this, Asari had conferred upon him the ultimate teaching of his school. Tesshu was forty-five at that time.

The swordsman Jirokichi Yamada (1863–1930), successor to Kenkichi Sakakibara describes the ensuing combat in this way:

---

*The *kōan* is a formulation meant to guide our meditation with the goal of reaching *satori.*[2]

†*Satori* is a Buddhist term for the enlightenment during which the individual awakens to cosmic truth.

The two masters put on their training armor. After the bow, they assumed their stance. Master Sakakibara held his sword in *jodan* [on-guard position with the sword held over the head] and Master Yamaoka also held his in jodan, but diagonally. They were about five meters apart. They looked for the right moment to attack as they let fly from time to time the *kiai* [a cry used in attack or feint]. The dōjō was calm. The disciples watched with rapt attention that was draining for them. The only sound to be heard in the dōjō was the two masters' breathing. It was a solemn and imposing spectacle. Ten, then fifteen minutes went by. Sweat ran from their feet to the floor. Forty minutes went by in this way. At that moment, the two masters lowered their swords at the same time and bowed. Then they calmly withdrew.

This was a well-matched combat at the highest possible level.

Saigo Takamori, a politician of the time, said of Tesshu, "It is impossible to manipulate someone who has no attachment to life, honor [concerning his name], social status, or money. Essential and difficult undertakings in the service of one's country can be accomplished only by such men."

Furthermore, all anecdotes about Tesshu speak of the uprightness of his conduct and his devotion to the path he had chosen. Such was the behavior of this man who had undertaken to follow the way of the sword in order to surpass or attain his master's level, an undertaking that blended for him with the state of Zen enlightenment. So long as the image of his master was present, his sword remained unconquered and he himself remained unperfected.

In Japan, the sword and Zen carry within them a classic image of man's achievement. This achievement moves along a path that entails the carrying out of certain codified forms that are linked to techniques and designated in Japan with the term *kata*. This word, which, as we have seen, can be translated as "form" or "mold," designates a sequence made up of codified and formalized movements that distill a certain social experience.

Katas play a notable role, just as much in daily life as in the practice of traditional Japanese arts. Although mainly developed within the warrior class, they permeate other social strata as well.

In kata, action is foremost. In addition, learning and transmission are achieved in a nonverbal way; speech has only an accessory role.

Tesshu's ten thousand daily tsuki are, in this regard, an eloquent example of the katas in swordsmanship. Learning a technique to be used in combat cannot, in itself, justify the severity of this training. In order to understand it, we must think of the process in a dual way: solitary training repeated ten thousand times a day aims for a technique that is immediately usable but that also constitutes a movement toward a form of perfection.* These are the two sides of technique in Japanese culture.

When the young Tesshu trained, he experienced his performance level, and, at the same time, his master represented for him an image of the perfection that he would be able to attain. In the rapport between master and student, the concept of a state of achievement or a state of powerful freedom or a state of perfection is essential. In whatever form of art we consider, reaching this final stage also means reaching a state of perfect human attainment. Certain masters embody this state. This is why Tesshu could not feel fully realized without being freed from the image of his master—an image that was proof of his own imperfection.

In the case of Tesshu, we see that the development of a strong, introspective, egocentric character was accompanied, paradoxically, by a deep engagement in the life of his society as witnessed by his absolute loyalty and total devotion to his feudal lord. In the ideal image of a man from this era, all converged to a single point: the affirmation of existence found its origin in the abandonment of all desire and the acceptance of death.

---

*The Western and Japanese notions of perfection are not the same. In Japan, perfection does not connote something absolute tied to the concept of a single God. It takes many forms and is accessible to man (see chapter 4).

For people of that era, no one felt any need to commit to writing this concept of the human being.* Tesshu's case shows us why. The guiding principle of his life depended not on a logical construct or an ideology, but on something much more pliable and much more difficult to grasp. It manifested through an individual's deeds without being legitimized by a verbal system. Nevertheless, it had a rigorous form at those moments when it was experienced by the individual, as if crystallized into quasiceremonial forms.

Nothing could be more ceremonial than the scene of Tesshu's death, for he met death in zazen posture, a discipline he accepted every day. Spectacular without being a spectacle, this scene shows that Tesshu experienced a time that inexorably distanced him from all those around him. It is in his body that we glimpse the bringing together of the two temporal modes of life and death.

The guiding principle of life derives its meaning from a formalized ideal that is outside the person, but which, at the same time, is internalized. During the Edo period, the warrior class sustained itself by interiorizing war and death. This movement of integration traveled along two paths: in the cycle of life, devotion to an individual's feudal lord (implying death), and in the day-to-day, giving preeminence to the present moment.

The highly codified and ceremonial outward forms of the warrior's life are intimately connected to this interiorization of death. Tesshu's life was molded around a set of ideals that took shape in outwardly constructed forms: in the way of the sword, it was the image of Master Asari; in the practice of Zen, it was a crafted form of life based on the image of the meditation posture.

By analyzing what the traditional idealized image of man covered in its relation to martial arts, I discovered the importance of katas and the complex structure to be found behind their apparent simplicity.

---

*During the two and half centuries of the Edo period, what could be called the samurai's code of ethics was committed to writing in only a very small number of texts whose distribution did not extend beyond the confines of the fiefdom that produced them.

2

KATA, OR "TECHNIQUE AND THE MAN ARE ONE"

THE CONCEPT OF KATA

We know that katas exist in all forms of traditional Japanese art, but their structure very clearly brings a much greater dimension that underlies any facet where words are unable to provide coherence.

We have already seen that, taken literally, the word *kata* can be translated as "form," "mold," or "type." Yet because kata has no equivalent in Western thought, the concept behind it remains untranslatable.

Martial arts, in particular karate, offer us more precise and more strictly formalized examples of the katas. In the realm of martial arts, the word is most frequently used to refer to the basic transmission of the art and to its learning.

As a jumping-off point, I would like to propose this short definition of *kata:** a sequence of formalized and codified movements arising from a state of mind that is oriented toward the realization of the way (*dō*).† In

---

*The word *kata* is also used to refer to the simple formal behavior of an individual when that behavior has become rigid. From this we have the expression "someone shaped with kata," in which *kata* has a pejorative connotation.

†[Readers might note that the ideographic character for "the way," (道), romanized here as *dō,* is better known to Westerners as Tao—the Tao of Taoism. —*Trans.*]

Japanese culture, "to attain the way" is to attain technical perfection—the perfection of a perfected man.

We can see then how, a few years before he achieved his final state, Tesshu saw Master Yamada, at the age of seventy, execute a single kata with his sword, and was impelled to exclaim, "So it is possible to go that deep with the sword alone! With this kata, we don't need to have recourse to Zen."

The execution of a kata is brief, apparently simple, and precise. In each art, there are very few of these forms. In traditional karate for example, most katas include between twenty and sixty movements. A kata is always the codified transposition of a real combat among several adversaries. Beginning with an initial situation, different each time, techniques of attack and defense unfold in response to the presumed moves of the adversary. All the techniques of karate are formalized in katas that have a fundamental role in the communication of combat techniques.

The tsuki that Tesshu worked on is a technical move, but, during Tesshu's teenage years, his master had him exercise this move as a kata—that is, deepening it and enriching it from the range of all of its possible applications. The tsuki is, by the way, included in certain sword katas.

A person works alone on a kata, focusing attention on the sequence while striving for technical perfection. Work on a kata extends over several years or even a whole lifetime, and it passes through several stages. That is why it is not enough to understand the kata as a group of forms or a mold, but instead as a way of bringing a larger field of knowledge into view. First of all, a practitioner must make a series of technical moves that unfold automatically. The goal is a perfect execution in the form and in the movements. In addition, a practitioner must bring to the movements a dynamism and a force, which are factors that contribute to the kata's effectiveness.

In the manufacture of a sword, the precise form of the blade and the hardness of the steel are two results that must be balanced in the artisan's craft. A kata is both the forging of the sword and the apprenticeship in learning how to use it.

Beginning with a particular situation, each kata indicates the possibility of a development and therefore brings into play the techniques of attack and defense in response to the movements and strategies that the practitioner anticipates in his adversary. This is why the various katas provide training in both strategy and technique.

A kata is not crafted by an individual alone, but also is the condensation of a traditional knowledge. Like the painter who applies successive layers of paint to his work of art, generations of individuals have laid down in the katas the sum total of their experiences. A very high-level karate master from the beginning of the twentieth century responded to one of his students who asked to be taught the katas: "I know only Naifanchin."*

We can be sure that for him this kata, which is made up of a sequence of about twenty moves, covered almost all the techniques that had been transmitted up to that time, and that he was able to respond to any combat situation based on this sequence alone. This does not mean, however, that he knew only this one kata. It means instead that he had distilled his entire knowledge into just this one.

This anecdote illustrates two important facts: The kata contains more than we might believe at first sight. Each movement truly is the "memory" of the movement itself and all its variants, elaborated over the years by a master and his students. The successive sequences of the kata remind us of the adversary's possible strategy, actions, and reactions. Its content, however, is not just a series of details. When a master and his disciples work for years with the same movement or its variants, it is the entire content of this work that gives meaning to the kata.

Although a student may train alone with the kata, the adept of a certain level integrates his combat experience into it—and at the same time, by means of the kata, he works out answers to questions that he has been able to formulate. The kata is in some sense a mirror, but it

---

*This kata, which began a karate session at the time, is also known as Tekki Shodan.

can reflect only what the adept faces. If, through the kata, the adept knows how to perceive the experience of his predecessors, the kata then represents for him a privileged means of appreciating his adversary and of knowing himself.

In the practice of kata, two aspects can be singled out: The first is self-instruction in which, using the kata like an alphabet, we learn certain technical moves that did not exist yet in our repertoire of movements. Second, we can round out the kata with our own experience.

In Japan, this form of kata exists in all the traditional arts, which means that the Japanese understand acts through the structures of the kata. At least, this manner of thinking was dominant during the Edo period. More recently, Watsuji Tetsuro wrote that in Japanese society there is "an ethnic tendency to trust facts only that have been understood intuitively and to disregard understanding derived from the process of logical thought.[1]

The kata represents a way of cultivating and reinforcing intuitive thought. In traditional Japanese arts, the aim of the kata is the same: to execute, in perfect form, a collection of movements transmitted by tradition—the perfection is brought about through the fusion of technical moves and a particular mind-set (termed following "the way," or *dō*).

The word *dō* is usually translated into English as "way," "path," "discipline," and so forth. Here again, however, none of these words convey the true cultural significance of this notion, because they reference it in a way that is abstract, partial, and superficial without conveying its profound meaning. The *dō* is thought of as a way that leads to a state of being that frees the human faculties in various domains of the arts. This spiritual state can be attained by plumbing the depths of a discipline. It includes an ethical component: to follow the way, we must follow the precepts that govern the universe and therefore society. The process of reaching perfection in a discipline—whatever discipline it may be—is an attainment of the whole person in harmony with humankind as well as with nature.

The example of ink-and-wash painting illustrates the constituent role played by katas in the traditional arts. Beginning with natural motifs—such as bamboo, trees, grass, or certain landscapes—models are developed. For example, in the case of bamboo, by bringing out certain lines of the leaves or stalks, the painted plant becomes "more bamboo" than the original. What's involved, then, is a form of perception and sensibility that is socially coalesced and through which the artist learns how to look.

This form of classical painting is learned through repetition and through following extremely precise rules. The artist begins with different brush strokes, paying particular attention to how they end, how they curve, how they fade out, and so forth, until he learns a perfect repetition of a classical repertoire. At the same time, the student works on a limited set of motifs from nature, using this same procedure of repetitive copying. This means that the motif from nature is treated in the same way that it would be in calligraphy. This form of painting, then, presupposes a homogeneous social vision of the natural world and a prerequisite consensus, which brings meaning to accentuated strokes, just as is found in the earliest classic poems.

So we find that there is an ideal model of the eggplant connected to autumn and of the frog connected to the rainy season, and so on. These models should be taken not as simple interpretative forms of the object, but as a referential base that evokes a moment in the cycle of life, with its sounds, its scents—in fact, with all the impressions that are associated with it.

The images flow from a life that is very closely linked to nature. The basic activity of growing rice is a collective work that is subject to the rhythm of the seasons and of life in society. It is subject to a collection of rules and takes place according to a uniformly repeated annual cycle. The images reflect a sensibility to collective rhythms, which, arising from both nature and society, derive an even greater force—one that is transmitted, in fact, very early in the upbringing of children. The kata is a formalization of this collective sensibility, and thus helps maintain it.

Yet the collective context is the arena in which an individual investment of self takes place, and as soon as a kata begins to be mastered, it goes beyond pure repetition. In this, the formalization is especially pliable. So the painter, as he draws an eggplant following the prescribed moves, executes a certain number of strokes that he learned by copying, but if the context has been sufficiently interiorized, he will outline at the same time aspects of the object that are connected to his experience of the moment. In order to be effective, the kata presupposes homogeneity of a sufficiently limited and sedentary social group so that a very distinctly differentiated repertoire of signs takes shape and is carried on.

Today, there are schools of ink-and-wash painting that extend the classical methods, applying them to motifs connected to modern urban life or foreign landscapes—but such extensions do not embody a force of expression comparable to that of the old models. One must look for the cause in the breaking down of the symbiotic relationship between the kata and the group engaged in expressing it.

Drawing its strength and its potential from the homogeneity of a social group in which communication is largely implicit, the balance in this relationship cannot help but be broken in a society where heterogeneity prevails.

THE TRANSMISSION OF KATAS

This transmission takes place in a homogenous social group that agrees upon a repertoire of coded movements. The initial apprenticeship is accompanied by oral instruction, but this is always secondary and is sometimes nothing more than a lure. The person who provides the direct teaching is not the source of the message. He only relays it.

The teacher or master of a martial art transmits the katas that he himself learned from the preceding generation. The origin of the message is hidden in the mists of time, and it has evolved down through the generations. The persona of the author appears through this mist, wearing a multitude of faces. Whether the succession of those transmitting the message understood it or not, the person receiving it immediately acquires at least the form of the message, which relates to the strategy of combat, ways of training, and other individual points.

In this message—somewhat like the language of deaf-mutes—the words have been wiped away by the passage of time. Through an assembly of trajectories drawn in space by movements of the body, only a collection of signifiers reaches the present. The transmission of a kata is writing in space that disappears as it appears. Just as a sound belongs to the moment of its emission, so too a move is attached to the space, which it cuts through and which closes back together in time. This is why the writing of a kata constantly disappears, but each time, it leaves its imprint in bodies that live at various periods in society. The evolution of a kata over time flows out of this.

In the teaching of martial arts, because the transmitters were not all of the same level, there had to have been numerous additions or omissions—leading to the kata being somewhat obscured. To recover its full meaning, we must rediscover its initial appearance by decoding this language of movement and mime, thereby understanding the intention of those from the distant past who transmitted it.

A single move can convey one or several meanings, because the writing of a kata is a series of lines traced by a body that breathes and moves according to various cadences. The lines are given their beat by the force of the body's speed. The dynamic structure of this writing makes up the kata. In martial arts—especially in karate—the role of body language is particularly evident; we might even say that it is fundamental.

For those executing a kata, the effort consists of incorporating this writing into their own body. At the moment when the kata emerges—dropping its ornamentation, opening into space-time—it morphs into a kind of living skin within which the blood of its existence moves.

At this moment the doer is no longer transmitter or instructor; he becomes himself the origin of the message. Through initiating himself into the way of karate, he penetrates with more or less intensity into this mode of identification, whether or not he is aware of this.

THE JAPANESE CONCEPT OF TECHNIQUE

In the notion of kata, technique plays an essential part, and the case of Tesshu illustrates the idea, common to all traditional Japanese arts, that technique is connected to a way of living. This can be condensed into the saying, "Technique and the man are one."

In order to attain an advanced level of technique, a person himself must become advanced. The quality of the person and that of his technique are in a dialectical rapport: they target qualitative attainment.

Quality of technique is achieved by incessant training, but sometimes the exercise may be repeated with no advancement, and then the adept himself makes no progress. This is how it was in the complementary connection between the sword and Zen at a certain period in Tesshu's life. The training intensity is an indispensible support for a breakthrough to a new stage. Then, the process repeats, following a development that spirals upward.

The kata is the means of development. It is a dynamic phenomenon that forges an alliance between the adept and his technique, not allowing the slightest gap to come between technique and the person's awareness.

What are the processes at the root of this attitude in the realm of the arts? The usual explanations refer to a kind of "Japanness," or a "Japanese soul," thought of as unique for reasons that are geographical, sociological, and ethnological. Yet it seems to be rather an extension of the animist way of thinking.

In each domain of traditional Japanese art, the expression *kami waza,* meaning "technique" (*waza*) of the "god" (*kami*), refers to a technique that seems perfect, or is at least close to perfection. This term expresses both admiration for and fear of the technician. He practices the art in a way that is familiar because the art is widespread, but at the same time, in a way that is inaccessible because the difference in level makes it seem unattainable. The simple fact of putting together the two words *god* and *technique* already seems to be an explicit indication.

Today, in Japan, animism is still evident in the Shinto* religion, which appeared during the rise of the dominant imperial power about fifteen hundred years ago. It is the first religion in Japan to have taken a universal form based on the life of politics. As the imperial forces conquered local tribes, their beliefs were incorporated into Shintoism by organizing the world of the gods according to a hierarchical scheme. The first document describing this cosmogony dates from the year 712 CE, and we see that Shintoism, by proposing a multitude of gods linked to natural elements, thereby integrated local animist beliefs that were also very closely linked to these natural elements.

Even today, the persistence of this way of thinking is very strong especially in the countryside, where Shintoism embraces many significant regional variations. A notable rock or tree, a mountain, a river, a forest, the wind and the sun, animals, different parts of a house, natural elements, all dwelling places, and so forth are still venerated because they are animated with the invisible existence of gods who may be good or bad.

When we consider the modern, industrialized face of Japan, it is hard not to be astonished at the persistence of these basically animistic beliefs. At the highest point of a tall office tower that houses the offices of a trust company, we can often see a small Shinto shrine that is intended to confer peace and prosperity. Before a new factory or the head offices of a corporation are erected, it is customary to have Shinto priests purify the ground and appease the gods. Priests are also present at the launching of a ship, for example.

It is not hard to see animist underpinnings in an attitude that

---

*[The word Shinto (神道), combines two kanji: 神, pronounced *shin*, following the Chinese pronunciation *shen* and meaning "gods" or "spirits," and 道, pronounced *tō*, following the Chinese pronunciation *tao* and meaning "way" or "path." Therefore, Shinto is often translated as the Way of the Gods. In other contexts, such as *kami waza*, the same kanji, 神, is pronounced *kami*, following the native Japanese pronunciation of the word. —*Trans.*]

encourages individuals to practice a technique with the kind of perfection that a god would exercise. Perfect technique, precisely because it is perfect, is seen as a god in and of itself—but the person who masters this technique is not like a god. The divine character concerns the technique itself, the period of time during which it is practiced, and also the being who applies it at the moment of its execution.

For the Japanese, perfection is human, and this idea is seen to be fundamentally linked to technique in each artistic domain: flower arranging, the tea ceremony, miniature gardens, painting or calligraphy, and so on. At the instant of the most advanced perfection, we enter the rhythm of the "breathing of the universe." In martial arts, through combat techniques, we achieve harmony between ourselves and the energy of the universe (*ki* in Japanese). Having free access to this energy means attaining the highest state in the art of combat and arriving at a new stage in our personal development.

From this perspective, the kata is not considered to be something subordinate to the mind: the adept as a whole is reflected in the technique, and it is in this sense that we can affirm that technique and the adept are one.

After the opening of Japan at the end of the nineteenth century, modernization introduced a fissure in this idea that humans and technique reside on the same plane. In fact, the kata represents an assurance of technical effectiveness if it is kept apart from any intellectual separation—the very separation on which modern scientific and technical thought is based.

The Western concept of technique subordinates these ideas either to art or to science. Technique is then a means. The split between technique and science developed with the division of labor in the capitalist production system. The relationship between the realm of ideas and the technical domain is no longer direct or immediate; it requires mediation and must be continually reestablished.

In Japan today, there are two concepts of technique. This is borne out by the fact that the word *technique* has two translations:

1. The term *gi jutsu,* which corresponds to the Western meaning of *technique,* was adopted toward the end of the nineteenth century and is used to refer to technique in industrial production.
2. The term *wasa,* mentioned above, is used for *technique* in the arena of the arts. In this accepted meaning, humans are present in the technique. In this case technique is not a means to attain a particular goal. Aim is not distinct from technique—we create technique and technique creates us.

Technique (*wasa*) is connected to the body. Thought and physical execution are not far apart and do not exist in a subordinate relationship to each other. Execution, when it is clear-cut, is to be found in a moment of intuition when the body and mind blend together.

Logical reflection is not absent from technique in the meaning of *wasa,* but it is limited by the mode of execution. For example, the artisan who makes a sword has time to reflect or calculate while he is hammering, but, at the moment of tempering or when the blade is being finished, an enormous amount of attention is required. The artisan must seize the moment when he becomes one with the object he is making. Similarly, in calligraphy, in painting, in sculpture, or in pottery, decisive and irreversible moments stand out—characterized by a particular kind of breathing—in which the doer and the object merge.

In a culture in which humans conceive of technique in the sense of *wasa,* it is difficult for the logical perspective to extend farther than the body's limits. In fact, the efforts of the human who wields technique bring together thought and action so that they exist in perfect unity. The Technique of the God can come only from this fusion.

When we say, "I have a body, I have a hand . . ." a separation is already in effect. This kind of formulation formerly did not exist in Japanese; it was invented to translate Western languages. This separation is not felt in the technique of wasa. Anyone who achieves wasa has to experience a total unity: "I am the body, I am the hand"—

moreover, "I am the technique, I am what is done." In this sense, the self disappears.

There is no doubt that this concept of human and technique contributed to inhibiting the development of logical thought in Japan.

In technique as wasa, we and our bodily movements can barely be distinguished from each other, and the specific nature of wasa can be found in the highly advanced, qualitative perfection of our doing.

PART TWO

The Emergence of Katas

The kata model is even today a directing force in traditional Japanese arts. The life of Tesshu illustrates the multiple dimensions of this model, deeply rooted as it is in Japanese culture.

To make these dimensions clearer, we must look at some historical factors. The development of technique most often goes hand in hand with an expansion of areas of contact and exchange in society. This is how it was for Japan in the fifteenth century. The decision to close the country to the outside world (Sakoku) was made at the beginning of the seventeenth century and was maintained until the middle of the nineteenth century in order to preserve social stability in Japan by keeping it in the closed universe of a very hierarchical system. The country was helped in this by its insular geography, and the social framework seemed closed and immutable throughout this period. Paradoxically, however, in spite of being deprived of the perspective of expansion or transformation, the activity of societal forces did manage to progress.

It seems that a process of interiorization and of returning to the individual affected all of Japanese society during the period of Sakoku. The kata model originated and took its final form at that time.

The Japanese worldview is rooted in an animist intuition that has helped shape the forms of self-awareness and logic. We do not find the same kind of opposition between body and mind that is present in Western cultures.

The kata, as a social model requiring total investment in an accepted and clearly defined structure, was brought into question only during the second half of the nineteenth century. When the historical rifts connected to relations with the outside world came into being, they were particularly irrevocable, because the social models were so rigid.

3

CLOSING JAPAN
AND COMING BACK
TO ONESELF

In his book *Sakoku,*[1] the philosopher Watsuji Tetsuro (1889–1960) attributes great importance to the period when Japan was closed. It influenced the formation of the irrational in Japanese culture, and he maintains that this characteristic is one of the culture's dominant aspects.

In a bitter tone, he violently criticizes this irrational quality and the lack of spirit in scientific inquiry that, in World War II, lead Japan down a path, which, from the beginning, could never result in a favorable outcome of any kind: "Men who scorn logical thought and who allow themselves to be driven by a narrow fanaticism have led the Japanese people into the miserable state in which they find themselves today. Behind this fact, we see an ethnic tendency to trust only those facts that have been arrived at intuitively and to neglect learning by means of logical thought."[2]

In his book *Fudo,*[*3] he takes this further and proposes an overall explanation of the specific nature of Japanese culture.

---

*This book by Watsuji Tetsuro (Tokyo: Chikuma, 1964) has had and still has a profound influence on how the Japanese think about their country.

31

JAPAN BEFORE SAKOKU

According to historians, the first structure of a state appeared in Japan toward the third century. At the end of the fourth century, at the time of the great migrations in Europe, this state extended into Korea, where a part of Japan's army had been stationed.

Beginning at this time, Japan began systematically to assimilate Chinese culture, most notably, adopting its ideographic writing, Confucianism, and Buddhism. By the beginning of the seventh century, the state was organized and provided with laws following the Chinese system. At this time there was no privately owned land; the land and the peasants came under the jurisdiction of the emperor, and the nobles were wealthy functionaries with military powers. With the pretext of extending the amount of arable land, the nobility established their property on newly cleared acreage. The estates that were formed in this way included both the land and the peasants. In order to escape the emperor's heavy taxes, the peasants sought allegiance to the nobility. The nobles then assembled very large private properties, becoming both landowners and protectors of numerous clans and local communities. In the middle of the ninth century, the power of the noble families reached its height, and one among them, the Fujiwara family, gained control and held on to it for three centuries.

During the period of the T'ang dynasty in China (608–907 CE), which was thought of as a model age, Japan enjoyed a period of political stability. From the end of the ninth to the end of the twelfth century, there developed, as it was termed by Watsuji, "a culture in which peace penetrated right to the core, the exact opposite pole of the violence that was raging in the West," and a period that was, for Japan, "its most luminous." This is the period when the art of Japan is considered classical, the initial flowering of which took its inspiration from the culture of the T'ang dynasty in China.

But already the warrior class was beginning to emerge. In fact, when the central power located the nobles in Kyoto (the imperial city from 794 to 1869), the clan chieftains, who looked after agricultural production and organized local defense, became independent. Their power derived from a flexible hereditary transmission coupled with a far-reaching system of adoption. This had to be backed by effective forces.

Little by little, the clan chieftains organized military force drawn from the local clans and finally coming to power in the middle of the twelfth century. The rise of the warrior class within Japanese society was quick, and the first military government was established in 1192.

Several movements of Buddhist reform adopted by the nobility punctuated the troubled period of the beginnings of warrior class power (from the twelfth to the thirteenth centuries). The reformers proposed a simplification of the Buddhist doctrine, which, in this new form, spread widely through the population. At the same time, Zen Buddhism, which suited the warriors' lifestyle, gradually spread through the warrior class.

The experience of the Japanese warriors was based solely on local warfare. Their range of activities was entirely within their own country, and there existed no leanings toward unknown lands—or they existed only in the idealized and gentle form of the Buddhist realm of Nirvana, the opposite of the all-too-real violence of invasions and crusades.

At the end of the thirteenth century, all of that changed abruptly with attempted invasions by the Mongols. Suddenly, the Japanese became vividly aware that there was a world out there beyond China, and this picture fostered a sense of belonging to their own country as something separate from the world outside. It was only seventy years later that the Japanese were once again to venture abroad with pirate excursions from the south of Japan.

The fourteenth and fifteenth centuries, the era of the Renaissance in the West, gave rise to a movement of the same kind in Japan. The literature and art of this elevated period became the source of new creations, notably in the field of song, theater (Noh), and the art of living (for example, the tea ceremony). Although rich in works of art and characterized by a forceful dynamism, the Muromachi era (1338–1573) ended with a century of wars as various regional powers began to battle a weakened central government.

Transformations in society, similar to those taking place in Europe in the same era, were indicated by various signs: the inhabitants of some cities organized forces similar to those of the warriors; migrations began to take place, linked to the development of manufacturing; peasant uprisings took place; and, in some regions, the populace came together and organized in order to fend off the warrior forces.

Initial contacts with Westerners were established when warriors and merchants ventured into China and Southeast Asia.

Two significant features, unique to these times, have been pointed out by Watsuji Tetsuro: popular uprisings (*ikki*), which arose in cities as well as in the countryside, and the movement of maritime expansion (*wako*).

Originally, around 1350, the movement of maritime expansion was conducted by pirates, who made incursions into Korea and China principally to commandeer slaves and rice. These two countries later negotiated with Japan and accepted opening their country to Japanese merchants in exchange for the reigning in of piracy. By the middle of the fifteenth century, Japanese sailors had developed a real import-export trade.

The former pirates, who mostly originated from the south of Japan, received support from the feudal lords of their region, which allowed them to extend their commerce into Southeast Asia, where they encountered Europeans. Later, in 1543, the first Portuguese arrived in Japan and introduced the rifle. In 1549, François Xavier arrived with the first Jesuits.

Subsequently, an armed force led by the feudal lord Oda Nobunaga began to establish control over Japan. From a series of successive victories over other warrior clans, Oda established a feudal military hierarchy. He represented a current that was open to the outside world. He was the first to use a large number of rifles in combat, and he greatly aided the Jesuits who, because of what they knew, represented for him access to a knowledge that allowed humans to dominate his world. He was assassinated in 1582, and it was his successor, Toyotomi Hideyoshi, who succeeded in unifying Japan.

Toyotomi set up the foundation of a stable government based on a rigid feudal hierarchy. With the edict of 1588 called Katana Gari (literally, "sword hunting"), he outlawed the possession of weapons by anyone who did not belong to the warrior class. In the area of criminal justice, he inaugurated centralized responsibility, which weakened the clans and favored the development of central control. In addition, he organized groups of heads of families, who together were responsible for the transgressions of each of their own people unless they decided to denounce the transgressor. This is how he tried to break the union of clans and local groups, which was the basis of the fighting forces of the preceding period.

After the death of Hideyoshi in 1598, Tokugawa extended and strengthened this policy. In 1603, he moved the seat of government to Edo and took a series of measures that allowed him to give the society a fixed structure.

It was only after half a century of struggle and harsh repression that the forces, which favored a certain mobility in the society and an openness toward the outside world, were crushed. Consequently, Christianity and the teaching of the Jesuits then seemed to be a political liability and were forbidden.

The final stage of this closing took place in 1636, with the Sakoku decree (Sakoku means "the closing of Japan"), which declared: "No Japanese person and no Japanese ship is allowed to go to a foreign country, and no Japanese person who has lived in a foreign country is allowed to return. Those of mixed race will be driven from Japan. Foreign correspondence is forbidden. The nonobservance of this law is punishable by death."

The only exception that was tolerated was the creation of an artificial island in the extreme south of Japan where the Dutch were authorized to carry on occasional and controlled commerce.

At the beginning of the seventeenth century, the pyramidal structure put in place by Toyotomi Hideyoshi took its final form. The social classes, between which no movement was theoretically allowed, were divided in this way:

- The nobles, gathered around the emperor, constituted a group apart that wielded no power. Their life was rigid and ceremonial and included a system of internal marriages that tended to ensure that they would be held within this closed environment.
- The warriors, at the summit of the social hierarchy, garnered the lion's share of the monetary income and were organized according to the system of a feudal pyramid in which each warrior had vassals but owed allegiance solely to his own feudal lord.
- The peasants were tied to the land and had no right to travel.
- The artisans and merchants were below the peasants.
- Last, at the bottom of the hierarchy, there were a limited number of individuals who were considered nonhuman, because they carried out such activities as burying the dead, cleaning up execution grounds, and so forth.

The distinction between the classes was very strictly regulated. The warriors were not only the ones who could carry arms, but also their costume and aspects of their everyday life were also regulated. The peasants, for example, were not allowed to wear silk clothing.

This organizational structure supported the development of a refined urban culture. In 1724, the shogunate's seat of power at Edo had a population of one million inhabitants; half were citizens and the other half were warriors, their families, and servants. The shogun required the feudal lords to live alternately one year in Edo and the following year at their feudal estate, which required them to leave behind their wives and children in Edo. Kyoto, city of residence of the emperor, was about three hundred miles from Edo, and at the time, it counted three hundred thousand inhabitants.

LIVING THROUGH SAKOKU:
THE RELOCATING OF INSTINCTUAL DESIRE

Sakoku, as a political tool by which the military government managed to secure its power, took the form of extremely strict prohibitions imposed on Japanese society at the exact moment when it was beginning to become acquainted with an extensive opening to the outside world symbolized by the Europeans. Its very severity proves the difficulty of going against this desire for opening.

The closing of Japan, imposed by force, was, however, unable to suppress totally the striving for opening—or the desire for opening. At best, Sakoku managed to hold it at bay. That is why it was ceaselessly maintained by the threat of coercive force embodied in law without which "instinct would force its way through into consciousness and into actual operation."[4] This is how the latent conflict between Sakoku and the desire for expansion persisted in the collective consciousness.

The Sakoku edict was bolstered by Japan's geographic position of being entirely cut off from the continent by the sea. The country became a sealed-off world where all energy had to be reinvested inside, and this total isolation of the culture—which could have been a retrograde movement—became the root cause of a complex psychological process of relocation and reinvestment.

The attitude toward the sea, long familiar but now forbidden, therefore became one of ambivalence. With its immensity having been glimpsed, the sea and its riches had provoked a curiosity that knew no bounds. But once the invitation for discovery had been forbidden, the limits of the world ended at the horizon. The concept of a world beyond the visible is based on intellectual reasoning and is to be found in a logical perspective that uses induction to move beyond the world's tangible limits. Sakoku meant a refusal and an abandonment of the vision in space and time that expansion represents. Because Sakoku could not be questioned, all human activities had to be carried out within a set framework. In order to accommodate this, the logical process of thought that was beginning to develop had to be abandoned. The introspective tendency of Japanese culture appeared and was reinforced at the price of this abandonment.

On the social level, society therefore underwent a kind of regression that forbade development while at the same time accumulating an energy, which, finding no other outlet—neither in the three-dimensional world, nor in the world of reasoning or technological invention—began gradually to turn inward.

The frequently promoted, irrational nature of the Japanese language is clearly connected to this two-centuries-long era when the Japanese lived in a sealed-off world while, during the same period, the Western world moved into a time of universal rationalism.

Sakoku was not only a political doctrine. It was also a way of conditioning people who strongly influenced Japanese culture.

> Prohibition owes its strength and its obsessive character precisely to its unconscious opponent, the concealed and undiminished desire—that is to say, to an internal necessity inaccessible to conscious inspection. . . . The instinctual desire is constantly shifting in order to escape from the *impasse* and endeavors to find substitutes—substitute objects and substitute actions—in place of the prohibited ones. The prohibition itself shifts about as well. The mutual inhibition of the two conflicting forces produces a need for discharge, for reducing the prevailing tension; and to this may be attributed the reason for the performance of obsessive acts.[5]

So we see that during the Sakoku period, instinctual desire was constantly relocated to escape what was forbidden in an effort to discover substitute pathways. The culture of the Edo period is characterized by a continual relocation of instinctual desire.

From this point of view, the transformation of the criteria for feminine beauty is a revealing example of the evolution of how the world was perceived. Wagatsuma Hiroshi and Yoneyama Toshinao[6] point out that

a considerable change took place during the Edo period—in fact, right
in the middle of the Sakoku period.* Up until the beginning of the Edo
period, a beautiful woman, it was believed, ought to have a full, heavy
body, a round face, and eyelids that were drawn out and turned slightly
down at their ends. Paintings up to the end of the eighth century show
this, and we find the same in literature, in both the novel *The Tale of
the Genji* and in the essays of Magurano Soshi.

Without going into detail about this evolution, we can see that
toward the end of Sakoku, the canons of feminine beauty tend to be
turned upside-down. In fact, taken one by one, the elements of this
beauty can be understood negatively in the popular image, still alive
today, of Japanese social norms. A finely chiseled face with the eyes
upturned evokes the wicked fox, cold and devious; thinness and dimin-
utiveness in the hips suggests frigidity and fragility. This beauty hangs
in a fragile and unstable balance with the picture of a whole that is
threatened with total destruction if just one or another element shifts
even a little.

This evolution of the criteria of feminine beauty toward the limits of the impossible reveals a complex and contradictory mind-set that
shows up in two cultural manifestations: theater and popular literature
and the aesthetics of *iki* (as explained later in this chapter).

JAPANESE MASOCHISM AND
THE AESTHETICS OF IKI

Contemporary author Sato Tadao,[7] by means of a series of examples
taken from cinema and popular theater, has brought to light a form of
masochism, which, according to him, is characteristic of Japanese taste:
"We can detect in the Japanese a tendency to hate the one who wields
an oppressive power and to love the pure being who, in spite of exceptional gifts, chooses death to counter this power."[8] This however is not

---

*The famous portraits of the women of Hokusai are from this time.

from an intent to resist the power, but "because these unfortunate figures, as they are brought to life in history or legend, conduct a resistance that leads nowhere."[9]

Two typical character traits of these heroes whose opposition stops in midpath are naiveté and purity—qualities that prevent them from opposing completely and lead them to disappear in a tragic death, which is the only way their spirit is able to burst forth.

The most popular of these cycles of legends, *Akoroshi,* inspired numerous films and is best known in the West as *The Forty-Seven Ronin.* * The 1962 version directed by Hiroshi Inagaki, *Chūshingura: Hana no maki yuki no maki,* is most familiar to Western audiences. Keanu Reeves will reportedly star in a new film version of *The Forty-Seven Ronin.* The Universal Pictures project is based on a script by Chris Morgan.

This legend recounts the story of a feudal lord, Asano, who, mistreated and insulted by a powerful civil servant, Kira, wounds Kira in the shogun's palace, thereby committing an illegal act. In accordance with feudal law, he is condemned to death by *seppuku* (*hara-kiri,* or ritual suicide). Forty-seven of his vassals revenge his death by themselves committing suicide by seppuku.

This actual event from the beginning of the eighteenth century was quickly brought to the stage, where it enjoyed and still enjoys an uninterrupted success. Sato Tadao writes that, contrary to the popular interpretation: "It goes without saying that Kira Kozukenosuke was not the real enemy. Instead, this old man is only a victim. He was wounded only on the forehead. . . . It was the government of the shoguns that executed Asano. So the discontent should have been directed against the shogunate. Killing Kira simply constitutes an enormous misdirection. . . . But the Japanese, in favoring the forty-seven, don't want to think that. They want to make this old man into somebody bad and shower him with their boundless hatred."[10]

---

*Ronin, literally "man adrift," referred to warriors who had no feudal lord, no work, and no income.

Refuting this view, Sato sees in the progression of this vengeance a kind of masochism instead of an example of loyalty. According to him, Japanese masochism explains the strong sympathy in all levels of Japanese society for the forty-seven ronin:

> The invasion of Kira's mansion by the forty-seven is in response to an impulse of attack and destruction against an oppressor. Following the event, their attitude can be summed up as: "Kill us. Our greatest joy will be to join our lord in death." We can see in the attitude of the ronin a typical expression of sadism and masochism, which are two sides of the same coin. This marriage of sadism and masochism is the shared reason why the warriors, the citizens, and the peasants, all of whom have opposing interests, can join together in infatuation for the forty-seven. . . . Since the Edo period, masochism and sadism are to be found at the heart of Japanese aesthetic consciousness in general. . . . What we have here is the most important emotional bond that connects the mentality of the dominant class and the mentality of the class that is subjugated.[11]

According to Sato Tadao, all Japanese aesthetic values in the traditional arts such as poetry, painting, calligraphy, the tea ceremony, and so forth are "the aesthetic sensibility of a small number of intellectuals who wanted to find a way out by themselves from the bloody and decaying atmosphere emanating from those in power and from the populace. They sought to listen to the internal voice of solitude."[12]

Sato Tadao wrote *Hadaka no Nihonjin* in 1958, at a time when there was a critical attitude toward traditional culture because of World War II. At that time, many intellectuals in fact portrayed tradition as one of the causes of irrational behavior that had led the country into war and ultimately to defeat.

We must connect this analysis to the study done by Kuki Shuzo in 1930, at the height of the Japanese empire, on an aesthetic characteristic, which he calls iki, which is simply another aspect of the same phenomenon seen in a different social context.

In fact, the two authors are analyzing the same cultural trait and evaluating it in opposite ways. This relates to an attitude toward traditional Japanese culture that swung in a different direction at the end of World War II.

Kuki Shuzo writes in the preface to his book: *"Iki* is a known phenomenon, but what is its structure? I wonder if, in the end, it isn't a manner of 'living'* specific to our ethnic nature . . ."[13]

The word *iki* is currently used in the aesthetic expression of the Japanese way of life. It applies as much to art as to urban life and has a complex, formalized meaning that includes both aesthetic and sexual components.

The analysis conducted by Kuki Shuzo brings to light certain specific traits of Japanese aesthetics and will help us understand the structure of the mentality that arose in the Edo period. Looking to the French language for help, he cites the words "chic," "coquet," and "raffiné" [in English, "chic," "coquettish," and "refined"] as words that are related to *iki*. "We cannot find a word that has the same meaning. So I conclude that iki is a form that arises out of an Oriental, non-Japanese way of living."[14]

Kuki Shuzo distinguishes three aspects of iki: "It is first of all a tendency to charm. The rapport between the two sexes is the original basis of iki. It includes manifestations of coquettishness."[15] It also indicates an inclination to resist, one "in which a moral ideal of the culture of the Edo period is clearly reflected."[16] For example, some of those termed *iki* are the city firemen, who dedicate their lives to the "Edo flower" (fire); the carpenters who, even in winter, wear the thin jacket of their trade and white socks without shoes; the pride of the prostitute of Yoshiwara,[†] who turns up her nose at the rich admirer who lacks iki. She will go so far as to die with her lover in fulfilling an idealized love.

---

*The verb "to live" is *ikiru* in Japanese.

†In 1617, the neighborhood of Edo where all the city's houses of prostitution were to be found. It continued to exist up until the 1950s.

So we see that iki is "a state of mind which appears both as a resistance toward the opposite sex as well as an inclination to charm."[17]

The third aspect of iki is a form of resignation, "an indifference arising from being detached from life. It is based on the wisdom of the person who has accepted his fate."[18] Kuki explains that "we come to know the real face of iki only when we find a slight trace of tears behind a pretty smile of happiness."[19] The tears come from the renunciation of a shared love and the smile, from detachment "which is a form of wisdom forged from one's individual life and from one's life in society."[20] And Kuki concludes, "To sum up, iki is a way of living in which the inclination to charm is constructed with a moral idealism and a religious unreality that characterize the culture of our country."[21]

In his analysis of this motif, he excludes from iki all analogies except parallels "which move along endlessly without touching . . ."[22] and have a quality of "resistance" and of "resignation." In relation to color, he specifies gray, chestnut, and blue, and he writes: "To sum up, the color of iki is in some ways the negative image that persists on the retina of an experience that had the tonality of flowers."[23]

Kuki presents iki as a characteristic intrinsic to Japanese society, but actually, it may be a cultural product of the Edo period. In fact, Kuki's analysis is limited principally to a study of documents from this time. If the notion of iki is an ethnic quality—as Kuki says—why doesn't he find examples in literature from before the Edo period? Quite simply, because this characteristic had not yet been established. Even though the roots of iki are buried deep in Japan's history, and it reflects a certain way of living, the aesthetic content described by Kuki did not appear until the Edo period, or more precisely in Sakoku society.

The etymology of *iki* has a relationship to "life" (*ikiru*), "breathing" (*iki*), "going" (*iku*), and the "inclination to resist" (*iki*). The structure of iki seems then to be a sophisticated intermingling of feelings and values, like the product of a certain warping. It is emblematic of the experience of Sakoku.

The internal energy that was endlessly turned inward by the closed and oppressive structures of Sakoku society imposed on the life of the mind a pressure that affected the smallest details and fostered, among other things, a relocation of aesthetic appreciation.

The complexity of the manifestation of masochism and of the aesthetic of iki was produced by the relocation of instinctual desire, which collided with prohibitions as soon as it reached the surface of consciousness.

4

KAMI AND JAPANESE POLYTHEISM

THE ANCESTOR CULT

The two oldest documents concerning the history of Japan are the *Kojiki* (712 CE) and the *Nihonshoki* (720 CE). Gathered from a collection that grew out of oral tradition, they deal with Japanese mythology as a whole and describe the genesis of the world, ascribing an important place to the exploits of the divine ancestors of the imperial family and continuing up until the formation of state government and the stabilization of power in the seventh century.

At the origin of the world, the gods (*kami*) Amenominakamushi and Tekamimusubi were born at Takamagara, a place of some elevation. Later, the god Isanagi and the goddess Isamami were born. On orders from the gods, they put a harpoon in the sea and began to stir it. When they withdrew it, drops fell and the salt, piling up, formed an island, Onokara (Pillar of the Sky). They settled there and created the Japanese islands and the gods of the sea, wind, mountain, and all natural phenomena.

Isamami died giving birth to the god of fire and traveled to the world of the dead (Yomi no kumi). Isanagi followed her, battling various forces, and along the way, he created three gods, one of whom was the goddess of the sun, Amatarasu, who is the origin of the imperial family.

The *Kojiki* and the *Nihonshoki,* compiled by edict of the imperial power, are influenced by the desire to justify the legitimacy of that power by attesting to its divine origin. Their appearance is an indication of the spread of political power. As imperial domination extended its control, local gods were integrated into this mythology in an apparent unification of cults within a hierarchy that left considerable room for local diversity.

The course of events in society depended on the kami—just as did the phenomena of nature. The forms of worship created to address the kami went hand in hand with the extension of state power, because all power emanated from them. It is the emperor, a kami and a descendant of kami, who carries out the ritual that integrates all the other gods.

The concept of the world of the kami, a world both hierarchical and abundant, formed within a patriarchal society in which the ancestor cult reinforced the tendency to impose hierarchy. The choice of the word *kami* ("high" or "elevated") when referring to the gods seemed clearly symbolic.

Within the religion set up in this way and called Shintoism (*shintō* means "way of the gods"), two essential characteristics stand out:

1. The ancestor cult, which played a role of primary importance in the stability of Japanese society;
2. The multiplicity and omnipotence of the gods, which brought stability to the existence of animist thought and continues to do so today.

The political and social importance of the ancestor cult is borne out by the exceptional permanence of the Japanese imperial family.

Why didn't the nobility and the warriors who were in power at various periods ever try to become emperors themselves? For example, when the Fujiwara family came to power and held onto it for three centuries,

Fujiwara established connections, through women, between his family and the imperial family. The Fujiwara could have become grandfathers of the emperor through these women, but neither Fujiwara nor his sons became emperors.

According to Watanabe,[1] the mythical ancestor of the Fujiwara family goes back to a kami who himself was a servant of the imperial kami. From the perspective of the ancestor cult, if a Fujiwara had seized imperial power, it would have meant a negation of the deeds of his ancestors, and as such it would have been the greatest possible sacrilege for a man of his era.

The same is true for the shoguns who were powerful enough to seize imperial control. They were unable to go against the continuity maintained by the ancestors that they claimed. Had they done so, they would have sacrificed the hegemony they enjoyed over the other feudal lords.

We must also note that in Shinto worship, death means not disappearance, but a rite of passage to another world—a world that is not far away and, though invisible, is identical to the world of the living. It is possible, then, to meet up with an ancestor's soul behind a leafy branch, on the mountain, or at the altar of a Shinto or Buddhist shrine.

Even today, when speaking of the death of the emperor, Japanese individuals use the term meaning "to hide." This is the formulation used in the *Kojiki* when speaking of the death of a kami—but it is also possible in this case to use the term meaning "to withdraw."

Until the end of World War II, for the Japanese, the emperor remained both a kami and a man. The Americans considered it politically useful to demand a declaration from him in which he affirmed that he was only a man and a symbol of national unity.

THE KAMI AND JAPANESE ANIMISM

In Japanese, the word *kami* is written 上 and is used to designate what is situated on a hill, on a height, what is located at the source, or what is respectable (on the social ladder), but also indicates the emperor.

The writing is made up of two parts when *kami* means "god": 神. Note the etymological meaning of this ideogram that was imported from China.

礻 means "object of worship."

申 designates both "the shape of lightning" and "the sound of thunder."

The ideogram therefore designates a "god who inhabits the place of storms"—that is, the sky.

Written this way, the word *kami* designates at the same time everything that is the object of religion, everything that has superhuman power, and the emperor. For ancient man, all natural and all human phenomena were engendered by the divine power of the kami.

The word *shizen,* used today in Japanese to designate the equivalent of what Europeans call *nature,* was imported from China. According to the etymological studies of Ono Susumu, before the adoption of Chinese writing, there was no word to refer to *nature* as a whole, and even long after the term was introduced and studied, the Japanese still did not always look on nature as an object. For Ono, this attitude has been carried over until today, because, for the Japanese, humans are participants in nature and are intimately connected with it.[2]

Within this view of nature, linked as it is, of course, to the geographic and climatic conditions and to the cycle of rice production, the powerful forces that seem to inspire fear or respect have been embodied in the form of kami. The forces of nature do not appear crushing, but they are capricious, and their periodic violence—typhoons, earthquakes—are beyond any effort to control them. The cycle of seasons is regular and very distinct, and when men bow before them humbly and respect them, the forces are beneficial and kind. In Japan, nature seems to be experienced as a constellation of forces—the force of the sun, sea, wind, land, and so forth—with which we must come to terms. The hierarchy that exists among them is in flux, depending on the moment and on the situation.

In its own sphere, each kami seems autonomous and perfect. We have seen that even today, in Japan, before the construction of an ultramodern factory, people still appease the spirit of the god of the land where the building will be erected (*jichin sai*).

This ritual is addressed not to the spirit of the land in general, but specifically to the kami of that particular spot. This attitude, which consists of considering phenomena both from their individual nature and as a whole, is the same in the technique of kata.

The survival of animist thought is often underestimated in studies on contemporary Japanese culture. In studies in the humanities, the main currents are those shaped by Westerners. Intellectuals born in the 1930s were very much influenced by patterns of Western thought. Further, in younger generations, the rapid postwar changes in society often severed ties with nature. Nevertheless, even today in the countryside, the Japanese have a Buddhist altar and a Shinto altar in their homes. Having spent my childhood in the countryside, I still have very clear memories of the worship of the gods.

During the years spanning the 1950s and '60s, in the morning, we had to bow before a Shinto altar, addressing first the god Amaterasu, the most powerful of the Shinto gods, and then, in order of importance, the goddess of the sun, the cardinal points, and so on, right down to the god of the toilets. We also bowed before the Buddhist altar and, on leaving the garden, the altar of the fox god, and so forth. On January 1, for example, we had to pray to the gods of the hearth in the kitchen or the gods of the water in the well, consecrating to them rice cakes or branches from a sacred tree.

RELIGIOUS SYNCRETISM AND WARRIOR VALUES

The formalization of Shintoism described above began at the moment it had to coexist with Confucianism, which was introduced into Japan along with Buddhism at the beginning of the sixth century. Buddhism was officially recognized in 538 but was likely known in the south of the country before that time.

At the end of the sixth century, Buddhism spread to Japan and began to exist side by side with the worship of kami. For many generations, the emperors were Buddhist, but at the same time, every year, they conducted the Shinto rituals intended to insure a smooth running of the country. These ceremonies at the beginning of spring were intended to provide a good harvest, and conducted again halfway through the springtime, to protect against illness. The kami of the wind and of water were honored so that there would not be too much wind or too much water, and later, after the harvest, there was a ceremony to bless the rice.

Today, Buddhist peasants still celebrate the Shinto cult of autumn, at the end of the harvest, with a two- or three-day festival.

The concepts and values shared by the warriors were developed on the foundation of an ancient religious wellspring of shamanist and animist lore and within the framework of a conception of the world shaped by Buddhist and Confucian thought. Because of this, when religious expression takes a more logical form, the force of this ancient wellspring is obscured.

The dominant value of the Shinto religion was the notion of *seijo*, 清浄 (meaning "purity"). It is a symbol of the god as well as the quality found in certain sacred and symbolic objects (ball, round mirror), and stands for the values of saintliness, truth, and goodness, along with having an aesthetic connotation.

For warriors of the feudal era, Shintoism helped to reinforce the ties of allegiance between the feudal lord and his vassals, but also it provided a ritual justification for the hierarchical relationships within each family between the living and the dead. Before going to war, the feudal lord, accompanied by his warriors, offered to a temple a sword he believed held spiritual value. In the presence of his warriors, the lord prayed to the gods and then predicted, following certain signs, the outcome of the war.

According to Motoori Norinaga, a Japanese man of letters of the eighteenth century, in Shintoism, all evil, wicked acts, natural disasters, illnesses, impurities, ugliness, and so forth were considered to be *keg-are,* 穢, the opposite value from *seijo,* 清浄, and the disappearance of all these evils followed the exorcising of this kegare.

The notion of guilt*—a characteristic of Western culture—did not exist in Japan as such. The idea of a mistake or a crime was included in the notion of kegare, but it had a meaning different from Western guilt.

The setting right of a fault by the warrior's suicide seemed to have a strong connection to exorcising kegare, and was carried out in a very precise way. It eliminated the shame that the warrior experienced.

Shortly after their introduction into Japan, Buddhism and Confucianism, which stood alongside Shintoism, were promulgated by the emperor, who drew support from their universal qualities. Buddhism spread first among the nobles, and then among the warriors, as they rose higher on the social scale. In the twelfth century, we can distinguish three forms of Buddhism: Jo do Shu, Nichiren Shu, and Zen Shu.

The first two considered that the world after death is more impor-tant than the real world. They became established among nobles whose fortunes were in decline and among those who suffered the chaos of war. They called for self-abnegation and absolute dependence with respect to religious values.

In the case of Zen Shu, each person had to find these values in the depths of their own selves, which fit very well with the mind of the war-riors when they were moving up in society. Zen invited them to grasp what is beyond appearances: "You must see nothingness in existence and existence in nothingness." Buddhism, mainly in the form of Zen Shu, led the warrior to meditation, concentration, adaptation to the situation . . . thereby extending the concept of life to that of the universe.

Last, beginning in the fourteenth century, Confucianism spread through Japan. It was taught by Zen monks who had traveled in China

---

*Ruth Benedict has written that the lack of an awareness of guilt in the Japanese is due to the lack of an inner movement of conscience in Japanese culture.

and studied Chinese culture, in which they played a significant role. Confucianism advocated the improvement of morality and human qualities; the search for perfection; and respect for and practice of rites, laws, and social customs. It justified and promoted the strengthening of the patriarchal social system.

Several forms of Confucianism developed in Japan, and in the seventeenth century, under the shogunate at Edo, one of them became an official course of study for the warriors. This teaching evolved with the social conditions. It fostered reflection in the warriors who played an important role at the end of the feudal era.

5

THE KATAS OF THE
SOCIAL ORDERS
IN THE EDO PERIOD

In any society, a child learns to organize what he does and forms his behavior based on the social models around him.

As a mode of transmission and learning, the katas specifically present a double, seemingly contradictory nature. On the one hand, they are rigid in that they are a structured sequence of bodily movements, and on the other hand, they are open and permeable to the situation and to the mix of feelings of the moment—which is designated in Japanese by the word *kuki,* meaning literally "air."

In Japanese society of the Edo era, belonging to an order is evidenced by the integration of a multitude of katas. This formalization into katas developed especially after the cessation of relations between Japan and the outside world. From that time on, each social stratum was caught in a gamut of rules and prohibitions that included territorial limitation of activity within a country that was divided into seigniorial domains. Orders were formed, and the warriors, peasants, artisans, and merchants became social orders that were impermeable to each other, thereby losing the fluidity of activity present in the previous era.

Little by little, each social order formed a protective shell that determined the shape of its existence. The individual could no longer move out of it, but if he invested himself in it, everything could take place within the limits of that circle. The collective experience of Sakoku* crystallized numerous social models into katas by giving each one a framework that had its own dynamic.

The kata, with its framework that strictly delimits its form and its reach, is a social model with a coercive aspect. Yet the framing also confers a feeling of security and, up to a certain point, plays the role of a rampart against the forces of change and the risk of destruction.

For example, in the education received by a child of the warrior class, practice in the many rites and respect for them were formalized into katas. Thus, we see that the child must dress appropriately in a kimono. The folds of material and the knot of the belt must remain impeccable all day long, and the collar must always be held tightly in place. The boy carries a little sword. Whether he is walking or sitting down, his back must always be straight and he must move calmly, looking straight in front of him. When seated, he must be proud in his chest and place his hands properly on his thighs. If he speaks, the words must be clear and brief and always to the point. It is forbidden to laugh under any circumstances. He must eat calmly, without making any sound with his utensils. Finally, when he walks in the house, he must do so silently.

To this education is added the study of martial arts and the study of literature, which is a tool for conveying dominant values. The result: the training, which depended on the repetition and integration of multiple katas, would be anchored deeply in him, and all of this would converge to one focal point—namely, how to die.

The execution of a kata, insofar as it is a technical model, is graded in a progression toward perfection. Perfect execution includes a limiting

---

*Sakoku here means not only the historical period, but also the social and psychological order that corresponds to it.

component: an individual could dress perfectly, but any addition would then serve no purpose and would therefore be impossible. In cuisine, for example, a perfect dish of raw fish can exist. The perfection is determined by the appropriate choice of fish, its freshness, how it is cut, the dimensions of each piece (neither too big nor too small), the color of its surfaces, its arrangement on the plate, and serving at the right time and in the right circumstance. The kata, then, is not the creation of an object, but is instead the totality created by one or several people in space-time. The dish will be perfect only if it is appropriately received. Perfection can be only in the moment.

We must guard against a simplistic interpretation that would consider the production of the kata to be identical repetition, for in the striving toward perfection, the kata includes an internal dynamic. Every time reference to the ideal model enters into the situation in a specific space-time and in the trajectory of an individual.

The example of martial arts, in which identification with the double*—both teacher and adversary—can become an obsession, helps us to grasp the psychological aspects of kata. In the katas of the different social orders, identification with an ideal image was based on the same kind of structure. It happened within a common, stratified, and diversified representation of society. There was an ideal image for the warrior, but there was also an ideal for the peasant, the artisan, and the merchant. Today, this still exists, but to a lesser extent, for example in the case of the student or the salaried worker. The leftist Japanese student or the politician uses an intonation and a rhythm in his speech patterns, which relate to a way of being that is distinct from the content of what he is saying.

Supported by the katas, the ideal image, inlaid in a representation

---

*[The French term here (*l'autre*) means literally and broadly "the other person or thing." Because English balks at using *other* as a noun in this way, I have chosen to use the word *double*. Even though it is unusual, it seems to convey the essence of the author's intent. As the author develops his analysis, multiple meanings or faces are assigned to the double. —*Trans.*]

of the totality of society, becomes a mold toward which the dynamism of the group moves. The ease of communication within the group and the resistance to social change both have their origin in this.

In the katas of the social orders, the effort of identification is not an individual matter, and this identification is socialized even more because the katas' learning and transmission are linked to membership in each order. As each person learns to structure his movements and his behavior in relation to those with whom he interacts, a perfect implementation of the kata allows him to determine his membership in a particular order based on the slightest gesture or the briefest word. So in the Edo period, the vocabulary and the articulation of words located a person socially in an irrefutable way. Each person's time was filtered through acceptance of his social situation, because life was directed by a very strong social rigidity. The position of each individual in the hierarchy was therefore very rarely brought into question, because the striving to move upward socially could find release in the katas of each order.

The education of individual warriors aimed to provide a rigid social framework elaborated in a ceremonial fashion. The warrior had only to devote himself fully to it. In this framework, the feudal lord was in the background as someone who could not be questioned. In all the instructive stories about warriors—and it is still true today—allegiance to the feudal lord and personal commitment were extremely important. Because this allegiance was to a single lord and was unchangeable, the commitment was necessarily especially intense. It was different from any other type of feudal relationship.

The ideal image of the warrior is best expressed by the way in which death is inflicted or endured. Seppuku is imprinted from childhood at the very center of a warrior's upbringing and education. The kata of seppuku is structured ceremoniously and would never be questioned by a warrior. Belonging to an order means not only acceptance of but embodiment of this model. It is never explained, and each individual learns his warrior's duty without asking why he would die in such a way. The sum total of his movements is simply respected and defended because that is what a warrior does. Tales of heroic seppukus are part of collective memory. The cycle of identification, which, for the warriors, upholds and brings together the katas, ends only upon the warriors' death.

The preeminent images of masculine identification, deeply colored with ambivalence, were imprinted along a series of levels with the feudal lord at the summit. Dependency relationships went hand in hand with a deep respect for age. This society was one of men in which homosexuality was not forbidden and was practiced openly. Loyalty to one's lord was connected to the history of the group because it could be traced back to connections that link ancestors to each other. In this period of stasis, ancestor worship, as it contributed to each family's continuation, was something fundamental. The perspective of time came to rest with the feudal lord of the moment, as he was, within his lineage, both in the past and in the future. Each warrior's life unfolded within this continuous and predictable time frame within which the katas were laid down. In this setting, paternal and maternal images formed within the permanence of the household.

An involvement that extends to an individual's complete disregard for himself is also one of the dominant values of the ideal image of the woman, who is to be found in the shadow of the man who heads the household. The ideal image of the man is formed around a complex outline of identification and masculine loyalty, while that of the woman, whose first duty is to produce a son, is dominated by devotion to the household—that is, to the man.

Without dwelling on this point, it is essential to mention two important aspects of the ideal image of the woman. The term *amae*[1] is used to describe dependent, passive love that links the child to its mother and the unlimited devotion expected by the child in return. The distinction between myself and others is erased and the relationship moves toward a fusion between the two. Amae is one of the bases of the formation of affective rapport in Japan.

The ideal image of the relationship between a man and woman is to be found in this rapport. What is expected of the woman is an all-encompassing tenderness expressed in formalized gestures that anticipate desires and in an attitude of encouraging acceptance. This very maternal image is reinforced by her role as the guardian of duties in the household and is accompanied by a representation of femininity with sexual overtones through similarly codified gestures, tone of voice, language, and so forth. The social horizon of the woman can be assigned value only insofar as it relates to the home—one of the expressions used for "my wife" is *ka nai,* meaning literally "the interior of the house."

In contemporary Japan, the emancipation of women began only when they distanced themselves from the home, but outside the home there was very little room for the woman in society. By turning to the outside, women brought into question the whole concept of the home—that is, the very basis of socialization. A denial of any transformation of the feminine image has been reinforced in many ways.

When the order of warriors developed martial arts, it was the manifestation of a life. Martial arts provide a key—the organization of gesture and movement and the techniques of the art give us direct access to levels that are the most difficult to understand. What appears outwardly in martial arts carries the totality of the life of the warriors.

Warriors did not participate in the production of material goods as their katas were being developed. Instead, they produced an organized form of society and the arts. This is why the kata of the order of warriors is much more than a sign or a symbol. It is the visible manifestation of the whole of their life. Their code did not need to be written. For them, under the term *kata,* then, it was justified to include martial arts, the course of a life, and the standards of a way of living.

During the same era, however, the other social orders produced something other than art, even if they practiced the arts. Actually, their connection to action and to the totality of their lives was not located in the same dimension. It did not have the same degree of cohesion as that of the order of warriors. When they used the katas as models, their social practices were more or less shifted in relation to their production of katas.

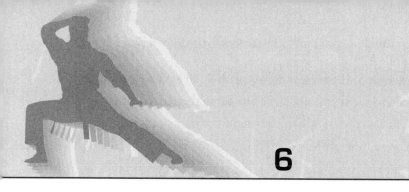

6

BREAKING POINTS
IN HISTORY

The notion of katas gives structure to the models that dominate the life of the warriors. Properly speaking, the life of the other social classes is directed not by katas, but instead by models closely related to them—which the notion of katas helps us understand.

We see then that the technique (*wasa*) that is found in the kata dominates the most elaborate craft productions and provides us with the societal image of the manufacture of an object of quality. In daily life, katas are effective when the territory of the life of each person is limited to the interior of a homogenous social group. Katas are able to develop and become a transmittable form of activity only within groups whose way of life is very much shared and where each individual is extremely sensitive to what the others are feeling and to the atmosphere of the group, though this exchange of feelings need not take place in words.

During the Sakoku, severe measures were taken in order to reinforce the organization of the population into small, closed communities. The mobility that was imposed on the warriors—they had to alternate their place of residence—allowed them to be deeply influenced by both their local group and the shogun's court. Along with their retinue, they were the only link between the two worlds. The merchants were the only other group who had some limited freedom to move about.

As an extension of the local group within the village, the family circle was the dominant form of sociability. The broad outline of this form consisted of the predominance of "us" over individual relationships; the extreme sensitivity of each person to the feelings and reactions of others; the fact that most often feelings are not expressed in words and must be guessed from implicit signs; and, finally, the agreement on collective decisions, taken unanimously. Accommodation between the authoritative patriarchal power and the hierarchical authority was never made by imposing decisions, but instead existed through a mode of reciprocal anticipation, each one seeking to feel the other's expectation, and always with a respect for rank.

Rigid, well-structured models integrated in individuals are clearly effective in such a society. By contrast, the process of modernization of Japan represents a break in the homogeneity and stability of Japanese society—a society whose horizon now has been extended to encompass a global perspective.

Individuals whose way of life was based on katas now find themselves out of step with this new society. Sensitivity among people is still present, but the dimension of the groups expands and the ground of shared understanding based on common experience shrinks. The break arises not from the local groups, but actually from the society as a whole, through its contact with modern Western societies.

Since its opening, Japan has remained aware, more or less intensely, of the danger that the West represents on economic and military fronts. When a crisis affects the country, it reverberates through every cell of the society as a result of each individual's sensitivity to the general atmosphere. Through the effect of a return to the global level, situations of crisis or imbalance in the collective mind are liable to appear very quickly. The kata model means that the resistance that any individual can bring to oppose the dominant social current is very fragile. Sensitivity to this current is made even stronger because the process of socialization encourages individuals to conform to the katas rather than to think logically. If the kata model is effective in a given situation, it can lead to acts that are completely misaligned in a situation that is global and heterogeneous.

Along these lines, it must be said that to understand the place of katas in twenty-first-century Japan, it is important to recall the two great schisms in its recent history, each of which corresponds to a reorganization of the country's social structure: the opening of Japan (1868), and the defeat and abolition of the imperial regime (1945).

THE END OF FEUDALISM AND OPENING TO THE OUTSIDE WORLD

In 1868, the beginning of the Meiji era, Japan embarked on a new phase in its development. The social structures of feudalism were destroyed and replaced. There occurred a transition from the shogunate to the state directed by the emperor, abolition of the feudal hierarchy, and installation of an egalitarian system.

Many institutions fashioned after those of Western countries were developed and formed the basis of a capitalist society within a regime in which the emperor had absolute power.

Formerly, the schema of Japanese feudal society was characterized by a strong cohesiveness. The domination of the order of warriors was based on a multitude of clearly defined territorial demarcations; people lived attached to the land. The system of hierarchical relationships among the orders was apparent in direct social relationships. The ideology of the warrior class, built with such strength, held sway unchallenged over the country's value system. This ideology was characterized by scorn for material goods.

By the end of the nineteenth century, the Japan of the shoguns, which was closed in upon itself, had enjoyed a long period of peace that had given rise to particular cultural forms. During this period, domestic commerce grew and increased the wealth of the merchants who were involved in exchanges outside their order but who did not constitute a group with any real power.

The warrior class, whose wealth depended on exploiting the peasants with their primitive production methods, began to become impoverished with the spread of a monetary system. The great feudal lords began to borrow from the merchants, and those warriors who found themselves at the bottom of the hierarchy began to experience a period of painful economic crisis.

The exploitation of the peasantry deepened, impoverishing a class that was more and more divided into rich peasants and poor peasants. This process was stimulated as a monetary system was developed and as merchants began to invest in land.

A feature of the development of modern Japanese society beginning with the Meiji era is that the mode of capitalist industrial manufacturing grew under the direction of a managerial group that emerged from the warrior class—which is why we attach importance to an analysis of the concepts and collective values of that class. The persistence of these concepts and values are immediately apparent at two levels:

1. The feudal relationship of dependence/domination, which constituted the substance of the hierarchical structure, was cut off institutionally (egalitarian legislation), but was transferred into a relationship with the emperor. It then became abstract and bilateral, but the range of values that it implied continued unchanged.
2. Hierarchical social relationships were maintained in the new structures, but with the exception of family relationships and relations between age groups, they lost their explicit ideological foundation. We can therefore speak then of collective values that were relegated to the unconscious.

Around 1868, among the numerous institutional changes that took place, these are notable:

- The power of the emperor replaced that of the shogun. The change resulted from a reversal of power actually stimulated from inside the dominant order. A coalition, led by both the less favored warriors and some of the southern feudal lords, took control, backed by the power of the emperor, and maintained a dominant role in the new government.

- Enjoying the strength of absolute power, the emperor became the head of the country. The government was secured by the ministers and was supported by a state apparatus (police, administration, and so forth).

- The feudal classes were abolished, the warriors lost their privileges (authority, feudal income), and equality was institutionalized. The right to bear a patronymic (surname) was extended to everyone, but it was forbidden to carry a sword, to have a certain hairstyle, and so on. Parallel to institutional equality, a new hierarchical social order was established, inspired by the Western model of nobility, and the former warriors now heading up the new state received titles of nobility.

- Private property took the place of feudal property. In compensation for their loss of feudal rights, the warriors received capital from a state loan. Most of them invested this capital in commercial enterprises—but, with the exception of a small number of brilliant successes, most sank into failure, largely as a result of their scorn for material goods and the activities connected to them. In general, the warriors had to find a new vocation in the bureaucracy, army, and police; among teachers; in agriculture; or in other occupations.

- The dependent relationship between populations and their feudal lord disappeared, and the system of control that bound them to their land was abolished. Individuals now were dependent on the emperor and could circulate freely.

- A new policy was defined regarding foreign countries: strengthening of the army (military service for everyone) and the development of industry.

We know that the industrial success of Japan was fast and remarkable. The rapid assimilation of Western techniques was largely facilitated by the Japanese attitude toward other cultures, which was characterized by a tendency toward superimposition and coexistence that can be compared to the process that we saw with Japanese religious syncretism.

One of the causes that characterized the relations between Japan and other countries undoubtedly had to do with the geographic situation of the country. Until 1868, Japan had never experienced forceful intervention from another country. Relations with China, for example, were limited to exchanges that had neither a military nor a commercial character. Because China was much more culturally advanced than Japan until the fourteenth century, the Japanese who traveled to China brought back models and know-how that were both technical and cultural. It is important to note that the relations between the two countries never involved more than a very small number of individuals.

The fact that Japan was never constrained by force to accept another culture is important from a purely historical point of view, but also because this was the reason for Japanese society's particular attitude toward foreign countries.

THE DEFEAT AND ABOLITION OF THE IMPERIAL REGIME

After the dropping of atomic bombs on Hiroshima and Nagasaki in 1945, Japan capitulated unconditionally. For the first time in the country's history, it was invaded by an army of occupation. Destruction caused by the war was enormous in all areas: Economically, the country was ruined, most of the large cities such as Tokyo were devastated from the bombing, and the destitution of the population was extreme. Social organization and value systems collapsed along with the defeat.

The allied forces were represented in Japan by the United States and the Americans, who claimed to incarnate democracy. They initially imposed disarmament and a constitution that was the most democratic in the world. In 1946, Japan had to adopt a constitution drawn up by the Americans—one that extended democratization as far as it could. Its preamble stated the definitive renunciation of war and renunciation of the formation of an army.

At the same time, the Americans imposed a public declaration on the emperor in which he affirmed that he was only a man and a symbol of the Japanese nation. This policy was clever, and even the Japanese Communist Party, which has been suppressed for a long time, considered the Americans as the defenders of democracy.

In 1949, however, faced with the threat represented by Communist China, the American policy changed: the principal enemy was no longer fascism but communism. The Americans then pressed for the rearmament of Japan and imposed the construction of military bases for the Korean War.

In 1951, the security treaty signed between the United States and Japan included the provision that in the case of war against communism, Japan would be protected in return for welcoming American troops on its territory. Following this signing, more than six hundred American military bases were established in Japan. The contradictions in this policy were partly obscured by the rapidity of capitalist development in postwar Japan. From the beginning of the 1950s on, the population, which had been living in great poverty, saw its standard of living rise significantly.

We see then that in the country in which the emperor had been venerated as a god, the emperor became no more than the simple representative of the nation—a change that was symbolic of the greatest upheaval in Japan's history. In a society in which the values of death and sacrifice had been the two main directing principles of education, the values of democracy and the importance of life became the norm.

From the perspective of the economic success and the relative social stability of the postwar period, it would seem that this radical change was well assimilated by the Japanese. Yet because a way of life forms slowly and tends to remain the same, it is clear that a society cannot change everything all at once. We are led to wonder, then, what it was that allowed this assimilation—at least, this apparent assimilation—of what was, in fact, a complete upheaval.

PART THREE

The Dimensions
of Kata

Through what process is the highest level of a Japanese traditional art achieved? What does that imply for the orientation of a life? What does it mean to have a master?

We are faced here with a process that is subjective and also very tightly delimited. This process develops during the whole course of our life. A transmission, a teaching, and an opening to the meaning of life and death can be found within it.

This process, which comes to the surface today in the traditional arts, is based on the kata—a psychological and social structure that, as we have seen, was formed during the period of Japan's closure.

Within the narrow confines left to them by the subdued population they ruled, the warriors transformed combat techniques into an inner art through a movement of sublimation and a return to the individual. Exercising techniques of combat with the sword leads in actuality to inflicting death.

The structure of the kata then depends on a complex play of identifications in which the relationship to the master invokes, far beyond a simple relationship of one person to another, the persona of the absolute that is death.

When the katas operate, they bring into question the connection between our conscious and unconscious minds to the extent that we can understand this within the traditional arts, the developments of time sequence in combat, and the way certain techniques tend to bring into question the organization of the daily activity of perception.

7

THE GYŌ AND
SELF-INVESTMENT

Returning to the story of the life of Tesshu, one question arises: in his search for the way, from where did his zealousness arise? Even though his life was unique, it was not really exceptional, and many of his contemporaries experienced the pinnacle of their art by searching in a similar way.

And today, how are we to explain the way Japan has succeeded in becoming one of the greatest world economic powers? Citing the Japanese work ethic isn't really an adequate response. The zeal of the Japanese worker—the way he applies himself—and that of Tesshu in his search for the way: might these two have a common origin?

The notion of *gyō* can provide elements of a response to this question. The literal meaning of *gyō* is "to walk" or "the walk." First used to refer to the practice of a person who follows a particularly difficult religious search for perfection, the term was later extended into the traditional arts, which, we should remember, are also based on a search for perfection.

The meaning of *gyō* is clearly illustrated by the way certain Buddhist monks practice one thousand days of gyō on Mount Hiei in order to reach the grade of *ajari* ("professor" or "master"). The expression *sen nichi kai ho gyō* refers to walking through mountain trails for one thousand days while reciting and contemplating sacred scripture. Mount Hiei dominates the vast expanse of Lake Biwa. On its other side is found the city of Kyoto, the imperial capital for one thousand years. It was there in 788 that the monk Saicho built a Buddhist temple of the Tendai school. From then on, Mount Hiei remained a central location of this school, and during each subsequent period of Japanese history, it played an important role in the evolution of religious thought and in its relationship to successive governments.

Even today, there is a Buddhist temple on Mount Hiei connected with a mystical school founded on a study of Buddhist doctrine and on the practice of rituals intended to embody this doctrine. Among these rituals is a form of gyō that goes back to the ninth century.

In order to move past the mundane level, this school demands that students subject themselves to feats of meditation that push the body extremely hard. It is not enough just to study and contemplate the doctrine; students must also be transformed bodily and spiritually. Moving from the profane to the sacred requires an indispensable physical detachment, because the true marriage of body and soul can be achieved only by getting rid of the weight and shackles of the body.

SHUNSHO'S GYŌ

Out of this tradition we find that on March 28, 1966, Shunsho, twenty-three years old, began a gyō of one thousand days. As he left the temple at 2:00 A.M., Mount Hiei was covered with a foot of snow. Shunsho was wearing straw sandals on his bare feet. The icy wind stung his cheeks, and the cold dug into him. He walked until 8:00 A.M., stopping at three hundred assigned spots to pray along the twenty-mile (thirty-kilometer) trail.

For one hundred days, regardless of his physical condition and regardless of the weather, he continued his journey. Accident or illness was no justification for interrupting his gyō, for such events arose only from himself. Any break would be a failure and Shunsho would be excluded from gyō for the rest of his life.

After his first gyō of one hundred days, Shunsho lead a monk's life, which consisted mainly of studying Buddhist doctrine, praying, meditating, and carrying out different types of gyō.

In 1974 and 1975, he twice carried out one hundred consecutive days of gyō, as he did the first time. Then, in 1976, doubling his gyō, he walked for two hundred days without stopping. In 1977, he also walked two hundred days, but on the 565th day, he suddenly felt a blinding pain in his abdomen. After a little time, although his stomach still hurt, he continued his daily gyō, expecting that the pain would decrease. That night, however, at about 1:00 A.M., the problem grew worse. Shunsho could no longer straighten up, and his breathing was painful. Seeing him breathing with such difficulty, the other monks were worried, but they could do nothing for him because it was not possible to consult a doctor during the gyō; failure meant death.

At about 2:00 A.M., Shunsho tried to get up and surmount his pain, but he was unable to walk. Two novices lent him their shoulders, and, between them, he managed to walk a few yards (meters), stumbling at every step. He still had twenty miles (thirty kilometers) left to cover on the mountain trail—a veritable Calvary.

It took him nineteen hours, instead of six, to complete this stretch, and he continued on five hours later for another hundred and thirty-four consecutive days without a break.

Right after this, tradition has it that Shunsho entered a temple cell and stayed there for nine days to pray and meditate without eating, without drinking, and without sleeping or lying down.

In 1978, Shunsho covered forty miles (sixty kilometers) a day for one hundred consecutive days, and then, in 1979, he covered fifty miles (eighty-four kilometers) a day for one hundred days, and finally, he finished twenty miles (thirty kilometers) a day for one hundred days.

And this is how Shunsho completed his one thousand days of gyō, having traveled 23,861 miles (38,400 kilometers) along mountain trails.

During the whole of this walk, the monk was dressed in a white shroud, because white is symbolic of death, and he wore a straw hat in the shape of a lotus leaf (water lily), in memory of the lotus near which the Buddha meditated. He carried a sword so that he could kill himself if he failed. Twice a day, at midday and in the evening, he ate two potatoes boiled in salted water or fried noodles along with, occasionally, a green vegetable. His only drink was soymilk.

Shunsho completed his thousand-day gyō in 1979 at the age of thirty-six. He was the eighth person to do so since 1925.

In our times, this trek certainly represents the most extreme form of gyō. It has been carried out for one thousand years and fully illustrates the original meaning of gyō: the process through which a man places himself on the path (dō) that he is seeking. In a form that is of greater or lesser intensity, this kind of approach exists in the various Japanese arts and involves a total immersion of the artist in his labors or in the practice of his art—as we have seen with Tesshu in the art of the sword.

INTERIORIZATION

The gyō seems to be introspective, but it is not oriented toward a focused goal.

The whole practice is steeped in ritual. Each step is more than a simple physical movement and must be accompanied by prayer and meditation. Body and soul are one. The state practitioner seeks is walk-pray-meditate. The form should be practical and unified, and it requires precision in movement and a directing of consciousness linked to that. The monk Shunsho conducted himself perfectly within his formalized routine. The gyō, then, is a way of practicing a repetitive ritual while following a process of interiorization and an engagement with our own life.

This notion moved into the realm of art when each discipline began to assume a stable form in the life of society and found its own specific place in that society. The gyō is associated with the introspective aspect of the art. When an activity such as Noh or painting took precise form as a genre, it offered the possibility of self-investment through a deepening of the art. Before that, because the form wasn't fixed, efforts tended to keep changing it.

In his works in Noh theater, Zeami* tells us that the quality of expression perceived by the spectator is a reflection of the maturity of the actor, which he seeks through inner work. It is achieved by simplifying movement and gesture rather than by trying to vary the types of expression. Noh actors work at paring down their gestures as they age. This simplification corresponds to a shift in emphasis. When referring to these stages of life and to the depth of expression in Noh, Zeami speaks of Noh of the skin, Noh of the flesh, and Noh of the bones. Using a simple gesture, the actor lets his way of being appear, and this is how we see his talent.

After having studied ink-and-wash painting in China, Sesshu† worked to establish this genre in Japan. Through a process of interiorization similar to Noh, the Zen search in which he was engaged shows clearly in his paintings and in the many Zen gardens that he created.

My analysis of the connections between Zen and traditional Japanese arts departs from that of Daisetsu Suzuki.[1] Suzuki assumes from the start that there was a Zen influence on Japanese culture, and he proceeds to study this influence on each traditional Japanese art. He seems to forget that Zen itself was transformed and reconstituted on a Japanese cultural basis. We must instead look at the common origins that shaped both Zen and traditional Japanese arts rather than assume a multifaceted influence on the arts. In fact, Zen is extremely different from the Indian *dhyāna* or the *chán* of China that can be found at the roots of Zen.

Finally, taking another example, because the period of feudal wars

---

*Zeami was the founder of Noh theater.
†Sesshu (1420–1506) was a noted Zen monk.

had ended, the art of combat developed when the practice of warfare was no longer needed in order to search for effectiveness in new techniques. Swordsmanship was then confined to a very limited domain, but it remained a status symbol for warriors and the source of their power. Training gained ascendency over actual combat. As training and combat tended to constitute stable models, swordsmanship no longer looked outward, but instead looked inward as it turned into an art. The aim was no longer to kill as many enemies as possible. The manner of conquest meant more than the victory. Combat criteria then shifted and became subjective, but this subjectivity took shape in a very rigorous social form.

Thus in taking on precise forms and in establishing genres of practice, art was established as katas. Only then could the notion of gyō be introduced into art.

GYŌ AND KATA

The gyō is actually a subjective attitude in the practice of a ritual or a formal model that is fixed and repetitive. It will always be found in deep practice of kata, but it is not a part of every kata practice.

In the deepening of a traditional Japanese art, the gyō comes in only when someone has progressed well beyond making the techniques of the kata automatic so that he can entrust himself to their automaticity. The gyō is an effort to go beyond the ordinary, everyday sensorial level. Whatever the realm, at some stage, the learning changes to marking time. The know-how has been acquired, and progress stagnates. The gyō is a way of dragging us out of this level by instilling a qualitative change of attitude. This takes place in the second of the stages outlined—when, after having learned the technical forms, the practitioner tends to use the art-kata to move beyond himself.

To form the gyō, when carrying out an act, it is essential to avoid dispersion and to turn inward. The rigorous discipline of limiting the form of each movement only to its precise, essential lines helps maintain this orientation.

In this regard, each day, Shunsho traversed the same path, but his mind never allowed itself to be taken by curiosity or by the observation of nature. He knew he must not be attached to what was outside or to investigation. His attitude was the opposite of inquisitive, which underlies any scientific understanding of the world. For Shunsho, the experience he lived through in his journey was a kata only to the extent that it constituted a world that he had to blend into rather than seeing it as an object. The introspective approach tends to unify what is taking place within the person rather than making it into an object. The integration is seamless and doubly subjective.

It is in this sense that the kata is formed by the subjective state of the individual. One whole aspect of the kata resides in a worldview to which we have already referred—one in which perfection is within our reach and where the border between the human and the divine shifts.

In summary, the kata is the practical, transmittable form of a technique for the transformation of mind and body. The gyō is both an act and a state of being. It sustains the practice of the kata while the kata is being deepened, and it enhances the subjective movement inward. This practice is meaningful because, in the Japanese view, it is by means of this practice that we can achieve the state of perfection. The dō represents a movement forward along the path that leads to this perfection, with the idea that traveling the path is in itself the goal.

THE GYŌ AND DEATH

Making progress presupposes that the path leads far, and its price is the effort of "walking," in the sense of gyō. Through a kind of self-persecution, we aim to perfect our own existence, while at the same time providing ways of maintaining it as we continue along the path.

In a very real way, we will surpass our daily, physical limits. There are other examples of going beyond the limits of physical effort—for example, carrying out an exploit, dealing with exceptional circumstances, or handling certain cases that are psychiatric in nature.

Those who make a gyō take on a difficult deed. Enduring provides the support for continuing farther. It is not appropriate simply to call this an act of masochism, for, to the extent that the individual moves forward effectively along the way, he transforms himself, leaving an imprint at every step. He must go to the very core of his being; anything less and he will never be able to see, to feel what he is, or to know the point where the mind and the body discover that they are really in symbiosis.

This endeavor can be thought of as a reorganization of the daily activity of perception and, in so doing, of our entire existence. In fact, we seek not a moment of enlightenment, but rather the practice of forging a state that lasts and can sustain mystical experience. What the gyō of Shunsho and the traditional arts have in common is the building of this reorganization of experience with the support of a structured framework.

This approach is reinforced and balanced mainly in two ways:

1. By a precise structuring of the movements, the techniques, or the rituals codified in the katas. This means that the body is directed by prescribed postures or movements that have been assimilated into our life.
2. By the development of a special relationship to time in which the interiorization achieved through the gyō and the katas allows the conscious mind to be placed in various subjective temporalities, either alternatively or simultaneously.

The notion of temporality in combat[2] can better help us to understand the state of consciousness sought in the practice of martial arts and often achieved in the practice of Zen. It is no accident that for those above a certain level, the followers of the sword have often looked to Zen in order to achieve a seamless integration of body and mind.

Still, the situation is different here because the intended result is lasting, rather than merely intermittent. What is actually involved is reorganization. The way ahead is clear insofar as the effort required is organized within a prescribed framework that is detailed and repetitive and is shown by our predecessors to have been effective.

The fatigue, the pain, and the intense physical efforts act as a support for moving away from an ordinary state in the body. This approach tends to break the envelope of daily life—that is, the corpus of life experiences accumulated from following the rules of sociability—and undergo other experiences that are new in how experience is perceived and organized.

The element that will determine this reorganization is death. Death will become more familiar in spite of its abstract aspect. It is an intuition of death that is sought. Going beyond perceived limits—such as making enormous physical efforts or the continual presence of the sword, which is there to put an end to our days in case of failure—represents the connection between life and death. The approach of death seems like a catalyst for the existential experience, and with each new effort, we see its reflection in the body. This makes its outline clearer still.

We must recognize that this approach does not tend to scorn and minimize worldly pleasure. We must deepen and reorganize existential experiences rather than deny them—as the relationship to food shows us. For Shunsho and his fellow disciples, food had to be frugal and simple. Seasoning had to be reduced to a minimum—a little salt—in order to allow them to be aware of the taste of the food itself. When he ate, Shunsho had to "unite" with the food he ingested. This had to be done with a fullness of being. It was not a question of tasting, which implies an appreciation—but instead, he had to enter completely into the experience of eating. Each experience, each moment of life requires the same total presence. This goes hand in hand—as we shall see—with an upheaval of temporality.

In the realm of art, the tea ceremony provides an example of a development of this way of looking at the relationship to food. It can also be found in Zen Buddhism.

8

DEATH AND TIME

THE MASTER:
AN INCARNATION OF DEATH

If we look behind what pushes the warrior's effort to unimaginable limits in the intense life of the sword, we encounter the image of the master.

Because the zeal with which Tesshu trained himself on the path of the sword is not linked to a real need related to his position in the warrior class, he appears to have been pushed by some kind of obsession. What is the need on which his obsession was based?

It is hard to understand how a child of eleven would repeat ten thousand times a day an exercise that requires a violent effort, and that after those five hours of continuous effort, he would train in full-body contact with his master, sometimes to the point of passing out—and that he would do this for five years. Tesshu practiced this type of training all his life, and relatively recent accounts tell of other examples of a comparable zeal.

Kata, gyō, and dō form a cultural setting that supports and gives shape to this effort. Those who pursue the path of the sword in this way seem always to be trying to surpass their own imperfections. We must remember that the perfection they seek is practical and very real. This perfection refers not to a divinity but to the very real and immediate image of the master who incarnates the form of human perfection to be attained.

Tesshu had three masters in the way of the sword: in his adolescence, Inoue; then Chiba Shūsaku; and finally Asari. The superiority of each master drove him to make huge efforts, because he could not continue to live in peace as long as a master who was superior in the art remained a constant reminder of his own imperfection in the way.

The superiority of the master is a form of power, but not one that is imposed arbitrarily. This power is to be found in a relationship of identification between the master and the student, for the master stands for the student's image of his own future once the student has made progress in the way. The longer this relationship exists, the more the power appears, and the stronger becomes the effort toward identification. This form of master-student bond is shaped by the socio-cultural context. At his birth, well before Tesshu was initiated into the way, he was situated within a certain structured relationship among men belonging to the warrior class.

Master Chiba died shortly after he defeated Tesshu, leaving him with practitioners who were not really superior—death, therefore, came down to his own level. When Master Asari defeated Tesshu, however, he once again found someone capable of dominating him, and who could therefore incarnate his own death. "As long as I haven't surpassed him, my sword is dead," he said.

The master is an incarnation of death.

Nowadays, death is often experienced at a distance, removed from the day-to-day and set apart. During the feudal period in Japan, death certainly had a very real, physical presence much more in evidence than today. All aspects of death—the act of killing, of dying, the corpse—were not as carefully hidden as they have come to be in our day. In that era, death was not covered up and had an explicit place in society.

Death is abstract when confined to the domain of ideas, but once it is strongly linked to the movement of daily life, it looks very real to us. For Japanese warriors, death was an extension and direct consequence of their skill. This particular relationship between themselves and death was the outward sign of their calling in society. It distinguished them from the other classes and had to be attested with care.

The idea of death was experienced in a way that was more physical than intellectual. From childhood, it occupied a central position. A common saying was, "The samurai must know how to conduct his own seppuku." The practice of martial arts was based on the idea that death was the consequence of a precise act: plunging the sword blade into your own belly and opening the gut by slicing forward, all the while withstanding the pain until the end arrives. Wielding the sword meant only killing, and because it was at the juncture between your own death and someone else's, the blade made death a fact.

It is said that a warrior of high degree in martial arts was able to feel the intent of an attack directed against him even before it reached him. If he was attacked from behind or during a nighttime ambush, a feeling would show him how to fight. Certain adepts trained themselves never to relax completely. Even during sleep, a part of the adept's awareness remained alert, ready in the event of any aggression.

Tesshu lived in this constantly alert state of attention as he strove to surpass his master. During the feudal era (Edo period), society was stable, and the relationship between master and disciple was certainly what Tesshu experienced. This relationship could be established only after the emergence of a well-defined social hierarchy. We can see that during the warring period preceding the Edo period, death of the most anonymous and pervasive kind remained somewhat in its raw state, and because of this, it could not be distilled into this type of master-student relationship.

With the arrival of feudal peace, death appeared behind the translucent veil of institutionalized feudalism and became more controlled. Killing techniques became an art—a warrior's art—and assumed a precise cultural form. The weapon and how to kill were crystallized into art by means of a metaphysical amalgam with the concept of dō (the way, the path).

Formerly scattered, death became concentrated into a dense, luminous beam within the cultural framework of budō (martial arts) and became embodied in the persona of the master who assumed two roles: feudal lord and budō master. The bond between master and disciple was reinforced by this, which channeled the energy ever more deeply.

To reach the ultimate in his art, the warrior is required always to lead his life in such a way as to remove any imperfection through which his art might allow the intrusion of death. In this warrior's universe of dō, any imperfection of mind in facing a possible attack would be considered a deficiency.

Death is metaphysical and concrete at the same time. It is metaphysical because the imperfection represents death in the world of his imagination in relation to his own potential vulnerability. And it is concrete because the possibility of an unexpected and deadly attack is real. When Tesshu thought that he surpassed vulnerability in the universe of his art, he encountered an irresolvable imperfection: the master. To go beyond the master's level meant for him to become the master himself, to achieve the ultimate state—that is, death—at every moment.

The relationship between master and disciple works in both directions: his disciples' regard for him sends back to the master the absolute that he represents for them. This absolute was partly veiled to Tesshu's students as long as Tesshu himself was in a relationship of student and master. When he reached the final level, the veil became transparent for his students.*

One week before his death, during a last, farewell training session, Tesshu challenged seven students and overcame each one. His disciples thought that the session would be a last chance to conquer their master, but unconsciously they already grasped the presence of death. It was death that they had challenged.

The master stands for identification with death, but at the same

---

*During a fight, Koteda immediately saw the change that Tesshu had undergone. See page 12.

time, he is a model of existence, of life in all its fullness. Arising in consciousness is a distancing between actual death and the representation it assumes in the master. At such a time, this distancing tends to fade, and the disciples find themselves confronting actual death.

EXPLODED TIME

During the Edo period, many warriors were engaged in the way of martial arts. This way allowed them to escape from the objectively locked-down universe of Sakoku society by seeking the limitless expanse of an understanding of the universe that was mystical and down to earth at the same time.

For someone who practices zealously, the search for the path takes on an extremely obsessive character in which the subjective perception of time seems to have a special persona and to play an important role. In the seeker, present time was not accorded the objective space of the moment. It was experienced as a superimposition of temporalities.

The future is located in time in the form of all sorts of subsequent attacks foreseen in present time, and it condenses around the image of the master: "Death is everywhere." It is made real within the warrior's body through the accumulation of learned and practiced techniques. By means of his body, in which the past is gathered into technical forms, he is able to withstand the pressure of the state of obsession. The body technique is a real sign of the present that wards off the dissociation that a superimposition of past and future on the present would tend to introduce. The present includes all the combat experiences that have been undergone and studied.

Within an expanded temporality, it becomes possible for the adept on the path to sense what would escape the perception of a mind in an ordinary state of concentration, for example an enemy's intent to attack before that intent moves into action.

The particular temporality of Japanese warriors can be seen in how they lived. Their way of experiencing death is the most meaningful illustration of this. "The thought of death is the first thing that the bushi needs to have in his head, day and night, from New Year's Day until December 31." This is how the *Budō Sho Shin Shu* begins.[1]

"If he is forced to choose between death and life, the bushi must choose death without hesitation. Death will always be the better guide."[2] Many quotations like this one can be found in writings on bushidō from the Tokugawa period. They show us that the bushi judged external phenomena in relation to their own death—which was a measure of their life.

If the master is the incarnation of death, what happens when a student reaches the master level? Life becomes perfect only when it includes death. It seems that this relationship to death must be thought of within a general interpretation of the Sakoku period.

The best way of concealing and repressing instinctual desire in the unconscious mind is to shatter the sealed and rigid societal structures in both their social and personal aspects. The warrior's way represents the manufacture in society of an object of substitution that allows the warrior to derive an energy that would shatter these structures. At the same time, the movement forward on the way tends to block instinctual desire ever more deeply, giving rise to the obsessive character of the activities that structure the way. The will to destroy is turned against the warrior himself, and the persona of death moves to center stage.

Obsessive acts represent a form of self-persecution, but one that is converted into a stable societal element that never reaches self-destruction, except in special, socially predictable situations. In fact, such acts always become established in an extremely well-defined structure: training with the sword or the meticulously prescribed progress of walking a gyō. This is true no matter what the activity may be: sword training, walking a set route, sitting under a waterfall in winter, and so forth. Self-persecution is always cloaked in technical garb or takes place with a quasi-ceremonial formality, and it is always to be found within a structured time frame. Integrating this activity as the way prescribes allows the person to move into a subjective temporality. Yet he will be brought back to the present by how the process has been structured beforehand.

In combat temporality, the warrior deals with the density with which time is experienced. He benefits not only from physical strength, from the techniques, from the *maaï** and the *hyoshi*,[†] but also from depth, intensity, and fullness of the time experienced during combat. The length of the combat can be a few seconds or a few minutes, but it is not at all a question of the exterior measurement of time. Combat time is subjective time, and we could say that we fight with the quality of our time—the quality shapes the combat. In fact, this time is not always filled to the same extent by our existence, which can be more or less intense from one moment to the next.

We see our adversary for a second, two seconds . . . ten seconds, but this doesn't mean that we see him all the time. There are moments when we do not see him even if we continue to look at him. The attack that proceeds from a high level fighter may happen when his adversary is looking at him, but the adversary may still not see it coming, even when the motion is not particularly quick. Judging a fighter's level by the rapidity and flexibility of his movement limits the combatant to a single dimension; in doing so, he misses what is much more of a factor: the quality of his subjective temporality.

In the reciprocity of time between two adversaries, time fluctuates between a presence and absence of awareness. It is for this reason that combat tactics are based on the ability to detect absence in an adversary and, as far as a warrior can, to maintain his own presence in the movements of combat.

A few quotations from masters of the sword clarify this notion of temporality. Certainly, these masters had no intention of defining

---

Maaï means literally *ma* ("distance" or "interval") and *ai* ("encounter," as with a movement). This term expresses both the meaning of interval or distance and the meaning of approaching or moving away.

†*Hyoshi* means the integration of cyclic movements that rhythmically link one or a number of subjects to their environment. Such movements take their place in the context of a cultural activity and progress toward a balance or harmony of the whole.

temporality as such, but they nevertheless explain mental techniques in which temporality underlies a particular state of mind that allows it to be reached and maintained. In this regard, Itō Ittōsai, a master swordsman from the end of the sixteenth century whose sayings were collected by his disciples, remarked, "Ma [distance] is what is most important to the fight. When our mind is attached to ma, we cannot respond entirely freely, by diversifying. When we are detached from ma, the ma is just right." Itō Ittōsai speaks not of a training procedure; he is describing an ideal state. This state of the individual is what the training aims to achieve.

Trying consciously to grasp the ma allows us only to enter a time that is locked on an object. According to Itō Ittōsai, we can flawlessly grasp the right distance only when we do it unconsciously—that is, by placing ourselves in what I call "exploded time."

In the *Gorin-no-shu,* Miyamoto Musashi writes, "In daily life as well as in strategy, the mind must be extended and kept very straight—not too tense and not in the least relaxed. For the mind not to be too much to one side, it must be placed in the center and moved calmly, so that it never stops moving, even during moments of change."[3] Miyamoto Musashi devoted his whole life to a search through the way of the sword. He expressed his experience of combat using images, saying that we must keep our mind at the center of ourselves, at the center of everything, and that the movement of the mind must never stop.

He interprets what he felt during combat, and he describes an attitude that allows him to react with his body before any conscious reflection takes place, in a way that is well-suited to each combat situation, because everything else is allowed to remain outside his field of awareness. During training this is sometimes expressed by "Hold the mind as in sleeping." This stance helps navigate a time that is not flowing in a linear fashion; instead, it stretches away to infinity. It is a matter of placing ourselves in exploded time or, in other words, of bringing together all aspects of the situation. Everyday time mirrors to some extent the flow of speech. By contrast, exploded time opens to a multiplicity of simultaneous perceptions and opposes the hierarchical constructs implied by words—which narrow and delimit the field of consciousness. Combat time is a time during which verbalization is no longer a privileged attribute. The image is elaborated after a strike in order to try to communicate this opening of awareness to simultaneity, an opening for the person who has also experienced it.

"Keep your mind centered." The habits acquired in combat maintain a direction that underlies the consciousness directing bodily movement. Locking onto an object or an aspect of the situation disrupts the fullness of this opening and throws us back into the strictures of everyday time. In this state of mind, neither the body alone nor the consciousness alone initiate movement, whether violent or calm, whether for attack, for feint, or for blocking. All movement is directed by the orientation of awareness that Musashi's images illustrate.

When Miyamoto Musashi writes that "looking and seeing are two different things,"[4] he is saying that in a combat situation, distances must be taken in without intellectualizing them. Instead, they must be sensed through the intermediary of the eyes and must be felt right through to the surface of the skin. Such seeing is perceived not as a spatial interval, but as a direct contact that penetrates the thickness of the intervening space. This sensitivity to distance can be obtained only by placing ourselves in exploded time. Then it becomes possible to "look to both sides without moving the eyes."[5]

Yagyū Munenori (1571–1646), master swordsman, tells us in his *Heido kaden sho*, "When you let the mind go, it goes away and often stays where it ends up.* To avoid this, when a beginner strikes with his sword, he must rein in his mind so that it doesn't remain stuck on the spot that he has hit. . . . In swordsmanship, our mind fluctuates with changes in our adversary. When he raises his sword, our mind goes to the sword, when he moves to the right or to the left, our mind follows him. These changes cannot be foreseen, and they leave no trace. Never

---

*As an arrow does.

having a place where it stops, the mind's trail disappears like the white trail of the ship's wake as it moves away."[6]

Last, the Zen monk Takuan (1573–1645) writes:

> I've been asked, "In what part of the body should the mind be placed?".... Nowhere. When it is placed nowhere, it extends to its full range throughout the body. When the hand is needed, it then makes the hand move.... We use the mind in place, where it is located, based on how the adversary moves.... Real mind is like water, while mind badly directed and stuck in one place is like ice. Ice and water are basically the same thing, but you cannot wash with ice; if you want to do that, you have to melt it and direct its flow to where you need it.
>
> This is why we need to melt a frozen mind, so that the water, flowing out, can cover the whole body. This is real mind.[7]

According to Yagyū Munenori and Takuan, to keep the mind steady, it must never stop on anything and must remain constantly in motion. When consciousness is fixed on something, it enters into objectification and, with that, into the customary evaluation of time. By entering a kind of total forgetting of the external world, the mind moves freely. It is detached from the temporality that is linked to objects, and it frees consciousness from the flow of time.

The exchanges reported between advanced Zen adepts are most often incomprehensible. Perhaps this is because verbalization is only a part of the exchange. Such an exchange is limited not to the conscious verbal domain of the speakers, but instead extends to all the manifestations and sense perceptions arising from their unconscious. The notion of exploded time helps us better understand how this relationship is established. Zen seems incomprehensible if we move these exchanges between speakers from an exploded time to everyday time. Zen monks, through their search, reached a state of nothingness in time; in achieving this, Zen provided great assistance to certain swordsmen.

Historically, the idea of the sword and Zen coming together arose in the seventeenth century and assumed great importance in this era. It gave rise to discussions on such questions as "Is the Zen monk turning into a swordsman?" Such questions suggest a certain mystification.

In *Tengu Gei Jutsu Ron* (Questions to a God on Swordsmanship), Master Niwa Jurozaemon (1659–1741) delineates for us the swordsman's way in relation to Zen:

> I asked, "Is Buddhism that is freed from life and death able to be used in the mastery of the sword?" The god replied, "The goals of Zen and swordsmanship are different. The Zen monk removes himself from life and from death by putting himself from the beginning in the same state of mind as if he were dead so that he can find eternal life in the cycle of life and death. Thus it is completely possible that when he is surrounded by enemies, even when he is torn to pieces, he moves his mind not at all. Yet this training is of no help at all in saving his life; it just means that he has no fear of death. . . . For someone beginning swordsmanship, if he doesn't train he certainly cannot find the swordsman's mind, even if he takes a lesson from a very great Zen monk."[8]

If Zen and swordsmanship come together, it definitely is in the realm of temporality. In his religious search, the Zen monk achieves a shattering of time, but in order to fight, this shattering must be channeled by a readiness to fight, which can be acquired only through long years of training. Someone who has practiced Zen can achieve this shattering of time, but he still must have the readiness to fight. The mental state of nothingness achieved through Zen allows only that the adept is detached from time, can move freely in time. Someone who moves forward in life by following a kata within the discipline of gyō is not lost in a boundless temporality. He doesn't have a body; he is a body that breathes time.

The state of persecution becomes destructive for someone who distances himself from his body—he will drown in the abyss of time, and the feeling of death will swallow him up.

The novelist Michel Tournier's character Robinson,[9] marooned on an island, loses his sense of time and descends into a madness focused on death. He is persecuted by his isolation; it drives him toward a break with human temporality. When his body becomes nonexistent, impalpable, he will be so lost as to doubt life itself. The body that has faded away in a nonhuman atmosphere will come together again when he rediscovers time.

> In this way, the level of the liquid always told the hour. The clepsydra was a source of immense comfort for Robinson.
>
> When he heard, day and night, the measured sound of the drops falling in the bowl, he had the proud feeling that time was no longer slipping away into a dark abyss in spite of himself. And, from that time on, he found that he too was put in order, mastered, and actually tamed just as the whole island was going to be tamed little by little through the strength of spirit of one man alone.

Moving in parallel to the loss of consciousness-time, Robinson descends into the abyss of death, which one day will lead him to madness, because he is completely defenseless when faced with the immense temporal expanse that death represents. This happens because he has nothing with which to defend himself against the shattering of the past and the present in his body. Death in the future and the vague sensation of the present life cannot be mastered by any means accumulated in the past. His body is vulnerable, and it will be completely denuded and exposed in "a stinging wind, like that of a pristine newborn child. When his body is engulfed in the immensity of time, he gives in to madness, because his body has not been trained to float in immeasurable time."

It is in this that we become aware of a fundamental difference with the person who embarks on a gyō. What we call kata is the form that allows a body that is working intensely to be contained. The form also protects the body, insuring its greatest effectiveness in the path that has been chosen.

ZEN AND THE WEIGHT OF WORDS

Zen is being considered here only in its practical aspect or as it relates to psychological techniques. The case of Tesshu illustrates three important points:

1. Zen enlightenment implies a qualitative change in the person.
2. This change has a tangible aspect.
3. This change corresponds to a reorganization of perception.

Old Japanese texts emphasize the importance of meditation in attaining a very high level in martial arts. Some master swordsmen have reached this level with the help of Zen; others reach it through the way of the sword alone, which shows that the two methods at least lead to the same result: an increase of sensorial acuity during combat.

The Zen meditation method is an amalgam of life and death. In it, all existential phenomena must be understood and experienced on the surface of death. In a sense, the perception of the world is double. In it there is a present experienced as such and a present brought into relation with death that enters into cosmic time. The precariousness of every event becomes evident when the event is moved onto a scale of time that goes from the past into the future, and as human existence is merged with nothingness. Zen meditation is meant to facilitate being placed simultaneously in a double temporality. In exploded time, consciousness, not being fixed on one point, oscillates like a wave between life and death.

Zen sayings, the kōans, are simply a mental training process in this reorganization of time. In a kōan, the question is concrete and understandable by the layman, and so is the response, but the relation between them is incomprehensible and devoid of meaning. Here are two sample kōans from Toshihiko Izutsu:[10]

A monk asks Master Tung Shan, "What is the Buddha?"

Tung Shan replies, "Three pounds of flax!"

Master Pai Chang takes out a jug, puts it on the ground, and asks, "If you don't call that a jug, what would you call it?"

The monastery abbot replies, "You can't say that it's a piece of wood."

The master then turns to Wei Shan (771–853) asking for his response. In the blink of an eye, Wei Shan kicks the jug over. The master laughs and comments, "In this contest, the abbot has been beaten by the monk."

The replies were spoken in the presence of the objects referred to, and in this sense, they are concrete and verifiable.

The question and the reply, taken in the usual sense, cannot constitute a coherent conversation, because they surpass the logical field woven from a continuous temporal perception. They are located in a more extensive communication zone woven from the double perception of time. The reply springs from the beam of consciousness that is found between the two poles of life and death.

Seeing an absence in the presence of a thing and vice versa does not mean logically seeing that thing from two different aspects, but rather perceiving it in a double temporality. This implies as well that one is located within this perception.

The inherent difficulty with the system of words results from the impossibility of producing this combination in one narrow and continuous stroke of the pen. Our perception of the world is social. All phenomena and all objects that we encounter are an integral part of a system of perception that is directed by an order of the socialized world: each is given a name. Touching my arm, someone asks, "What is it?" By replying, "It is my arm," I represent to myself the experience undergone by "my arm," thus moving it into socio-cultural knowledge. An arm is there, without me paying attention to the resonance of the sensation in my body. As soon as I have designated this experience by the word *arm,* my perception has submitted to a limitation, because the light of this knowledge is a centered beam. When the perception is linked closely to the system of words, it moves in a humanized and socialized temporality. It is controlled by logical time.

By bringing into play and overturning time's uniqueness, Zen meditation aims for a reorganization of perception that allows us to perceive fully what bypasses our nominal perception. Zen does not call on intellectual knowledge that has its basis in a theory or a rationale. Instead, it sets out to break down the framework of centralized, systematic thought so that, using a series of exercises, it can build a fresh spontaneity or intuitive recognition of broader scope. When life and death are brought together in consciousness, there is no room for words. Language has contributed to bringing a more or less rigorous order to the world, but here it is overturned and even driven out of the mind. In fact, in the state of Zen meditation, consciousness is detached from the thread of time that gives language its structure, so that instead it is connected to the immediacy of each moment.

Zen negates the logic of language, because meditation ceaselessly propels us toward an overturning of the world in our consciousness. Logical structures must inevitably dissolve in it, because life is not separate from death. Both life and death must be experienced as concrete and abstract simultaneously.

The degree to which language is rational is linked to the structure provided by consciousness based on what is experienced and on the concept of life and death. In our rational societies, death is cleverly interred. It is not excluded from rational thought, but it does tend to be in the actual perception of life. Further, though everyone knows that we all will die one day, death remains a mystery.

Life and death are like two sides of a leaf, and our eyes see only one side. Our reason knows that the other side exists, but it does not allow us to see both at the same time. Even though our eyes have this limitation, a leaf still exists as such with both its sides.

9

THE PSYCHOLOGICAL ASPECT OF KATA

THE MANY FACES OF THE DOUBLE AND TECHNICAL AWARENESS

When someone is doing a kata alone, the double is always still there, psychologically. This is what makes a kata different from a simple codified sequence of moves. The strength of this feeling varies according to the type of technical sequence that underlies the kata.

As the kata is carried out, the depth and meaningfulness that an individual achieves and experiences depends not only on the apparent degree of perfection, but, more important, on the intensity and range of an individual's mental state at that moment.

Criteria for perfection in the moves vary according to the degree of mastery of the person observing them. In each domain, perfection is graded in relation to the technical effectiveness that it reflects. That is why it depends on observations that are not just "well conducted," "well done," or "harmonious." What is actually an attainment of perfection could be seen as a lack or an imperfection in the eyes of observers from outside the discipline in question. Conversely, when katas are presented in public—as has been the case for karate for half a century—a change is brought into play by this theatricality, and the sequences begin to include moves that have no use but are pleasing to the uninitiated public.

We must be very clear that when we speak of katas in dance or in Noh theater, the double in question is neither the public nor the partner but an interiorization. The image of this double may vary, but it is always a model that leads to perfection.

For Tesshu, this image was an image of the master. He found its presence crushing, but he identified with it—and at the same time, he struggled to be victorious against it. When the potter making his vase follows the best traditional technique, he is not executing a kata. Instead, his doing becomes a kata when a dynamic series of identifications takes place in him so that the object he is shaping and the image of the master's movement produce the perfect image of his object. His moves are then impregnated with this image of the master as a precursor and as a guide toward perfection.

The example of Miyamoto Musashi, the master swordsman of the seventeenth century, allows us to see that the underlying psychological nature of the katas is the same from one discipline to the next. Famous for his many victories, Musashi attained the greatest perfection in swordsmanship:

> I was trained in the way of strategy from childhood on, and at the age of thirteen, I was beaten for the first time in a duel. . . .
>
> I continued to train, and from morning to night, I sought the deepest clarity. At the age of fifty, I found myself naturally on the way of strategy.
>
> Since that day, I live without needing to investigate the way any further. When I apply the clarity of strategy to the way of various arts and crafts, I no longer need a master in any of these disciplines.[1]

Indeed, Musashi excelled to the same extent in painting, calligraphy, poetry, and the tea ceremony. Anecdotes show that the state of mind forged by his practice of the sword had penetrated his whole way of life and affected not only his practice of the arts, but also the way he walked, slept, and so forth.

According to the documents that have come down to us, Musashi did not have a swordsmanship master; rather, he developed himself alone, by meetings and contests with warriors and masters. In the seventeenth century, the art of swordsmanship was very different from what Tesshu had known. In this war-torn era, the duels were merciless, training was conducted without any kind of protection, and the handling of the sword had not yet become an art. Musashi could not have received a technique ritualized with katas. He founded his art by surviving.

By the time he created his swordsmanship school, society had changed: a feudal peace had been established, and it was no longer possible to progress in the way of the sword on your own through combat experience. In his daily training, Musashi took his experience and gave it form. In his teaching, he tried to transmit his experience by setting it into technical sequences, which gave rise to training katas. At the same time, his efforts in elaborating the art of swordsmanship were being set down in books, the best known of which is *Gorin-no-sho* (Writings on the Five Elements).[2]

Musashi's many detailed recommendations derive from a reorganization of the attention. This reorganization is of the same type as that of a kata, because, at every moment, he experiences a connection to the adversary that he has brought within himself. In order to "follow the way," he places himself in a state analogous to that experienced during an assault engaging several enemies.

During the Edo period, this way of being became a key element in a warrior's training, and toward the end of the period, it began to be written in a codified form. Related to this, we see that while Minamoto Sugane[3] provides technical advice in swordsmanship using a great deal of careful precision, he also provides a great many indications on the conduct that a warrior should adopt. These indications show to what an extent this education can determine the smallest details of daily life, so that a warrior's life exists in permanent relationship with his virtual enemy:

In whatever location you find yourself when with several others, you must immediately take note of where the weapons are placed and where the door is. You mustn't be concerned only about weapons. . . .

Even with intimate friends, you must take care to have close by a pillow or a smoking tray that you can use (as a shield) if you need to, without being obvious about this precaution. . . .

When you put your sword down in a room, make sure the handle is always near your right hand. . . .

When you pass by someone, have him pass on your right (the sword being carried on the left side).[4]

The mastery of the tensions that arise from the permanent presence of the imaginary enemy is one of the elements of the warrior mind.

Another dominant trait of his psychology is illustrated by Musashi's indications in his chapter State of Mind in Martial Arts:

In the science of martial arts, the state of mind should remain the same as normal. In ordinary circumstances as well as when practicing martial arts, let there be no change at all—with the mind open and direct, neither tense nor lax. Centering the mind so that there is no imbalance, calmly relax your mind and savor this moment of ease thoroughly so that the relaxation does not stop its relaxation even for an instant. Even when still, your mind is not still; even when hurried, your mind is not hurried. The mind is not dragged by the body; the body is not dragged by the mind.[5]

The orientation of the mind at the moment a kata is performed proceeds from a technique that Zen and the traditional Japanese arts have in common. Behind the outward form of the kata, there is a working of the mind that tends to expand and relocate the opening and the depth of the consciousness field—as it is in the motionless posture of zazen. The depth and reach of the state of consciousness varies according to the level of perfection of the zazen, but although the posture—which is very important—is visible, the state of consciousness, on the contrary, is not.

In zazen discipline, each person knows that what is important is not visible from the outside, whereas in the kata of martial arts, the forms and the moves are apparent and give the impression that the perfection of the kata is visible. This is true to a certain extent, but in looking at external forms because it facilitates practice, it is easy to fall into the trap of seeing only what is visible.

When martial arts, in particular karate, are organized as a competitive sport with assigned grades, the psychological side of the training is completely misunderstood. During training, a state of consciousness is forged by a centripetal effort of attention, by an effort of introspection in the moves, and by an internal observation of the body's dynamics. When the physical effort varies in tension, force, speed, and so forth, the adept must maintain a quiet attention as he extends the area observed. It is easy to say this, but managing to get to this point requires continuous training.

If the adept encounters an unexpected resistance when carrying out a move that he knows, his perception is subjected to a disturbance that very often remains subconscious. A pain or an unaccustomed shock can amplify what has taken place. Anxiety floods in when he loses touch with an accurate evaluation of the facts.

When practicing firing a pistol, the beginner does well on the first shot and encounters difficulties with the second. What happens is that he interiorizes the firing: the shock, the noise, and hitting the target. The combination of these anticipations connect to the movement of pressing the trigger, and they give rise to a disturbance in the delicate movement of his finger. The learning consists of not letting this anticipation influence the dynamic of firing. Firing emotionally throws off aim and makes the adept lose his technical accuracy.

In a combat situation, anticipating pain and shock prevents the warrior from judging with precision the blows that he might receive from feet, fists, or sword. He must distinguish shock and pain from the anxiety that wells up afterward. An accurate assessment of the state of the body will help him avoid dramatizing the situation. It is hard to separate pain and anxiety. Once we have gone beyond a clear assessment of pain and shock, fear enters, anxiety is close by, and our overview of the whole situation becomes distorted.

It is very easy to say this on paper, and also to believe that we have understood it, but training involves coming to this state in a living body. When an adept learns martial arts in Japan, this point is constantly stressed without ever being stated explicitly.

The quiet mind widely deployed or the transition to exploded time must be strengthened through action. The state of consciousness must be able to resist changes in the situation. Simply arriving at this state when seated is of no help to martial arts. . . . The adept must maintain this state in a combat situation.

Yagyū Munenori, a master swordsman of the seventeenth century, advocated this kind of search: "Direct the body without being influenced by the mind, and the mind without being influenced by the body." The student must imagine that, while he is executing a series of rhythmic movements, he is hit suddenly or violently. We can understand how difficult it is to maintain the rhythmic state of consciousness at the moment of the blow. Training in kata allows the body movement to respond immediately to such an interruption without the blow affecting the inner rhythm.

The interval that exists during the movement leading up to an attack (its path, the intention to attack that precedes the movement) appears to the experienced eye of the adversary as a moment of vulnerability. In combat, the goal is to fill these moments of vulnerability without letting up on the intensity of the attack. The warrior does this by making his awareness and the movement coincide—but without allowing the mind to become polarized on the movement. It is very difficult work.

If at any given moment the awareness is fixed on a point, the subsequent attack can come from any of the other possible points. Being sensitive to these possibilities is a permanent inner critical faculty; in kata, we have called this "the eye of the double." The moment a fighter feels his movement begin, he centers himself in the awareness of an *I* that is related to his context. Doing this, he returns to an everyday perception, and his consciousness is directed by a separation between the *I* and the outer world. Japanese martial arts are an ongoing learning process within an awareness that surveys the full range of what is possible.*

In kata, the double is not only a fictitious adversary—this double can also simultaneously be an adversary, master, and masters of former times. Feeling this multiple presence is the clearest indication of reaching the mental state that we seek in the kata. This is why, on occasion, deepening a kata allows us to become aware of directives from the distant past that may sometimes be in conflict with the training we have actually received. It is as if a quiet voice says, "That's not the intention I transmitted with this kata; this is the intention."

Further, because the double is at the same time an adversary, fighting him brings his experience to bear and develops our knowledge. Throughout the kata, awareness must be held in a kind of unrestricted opening that assists entry into exploded time. As soon as a word or a specific image arises, the attention is affected and becomes limited. We must avoid stopping on a thought or a sensation so that we are not brought back into channeled time.

Exploded time is not like a point or a flash; it is a state of consciousness that has depth and breadth, a technical awareness that opens into a critical faculty that is right here and present at every moment. This critical faculty comes through the multiple personae of the double when we are alone, and through the adversary when we are actually in his presence. We are therefore speaking not of a purely subjective state. The critical faculty that includes a dynamic relationship with the adversary continually breaks down subjectivity.

Today, even within the limited realm of art, effectiveness remains nonetheless the determining factor in the development of this awareness.

---

*In the teaching of martial arts, there is an insistence on *mu-ga* (non-I).

In archery, explanations are useless if the arrow misses the target. In swordsmanship, the strike that moves out and follows through just as it should, without anything being decided in the moment, is one of the signs confirming that the desired state has been achieved.

A LIFE KATA

Karate master Gichin Funakoshi (1868–1958) wrote in his *Twenty Precepts for the Way of Karate*: "You need to transform into karate all of the phenomena of your life."[6]

This precept does not tell us to put our attention all the time on combat technique. Instead, it says that we must adopt the open state of mind that is characteristic of the kata across the broadest possible range of circumstances.

As we have defined them up to this point, katas are fixed within an art as a moment that is precise and circumscribed. Yet the observable mental structure in a kata may expand and become the dominant element of a personality. When an adept experiences every event in relation to karate, his whole life becomes structured along the lines of the specific kata of karate, in the way that Tesshu's life was structured in the kata of the sword. This type of kata, with its existential dynamic, can be called a life kata.

In martial arts, life becomes structured as a kata if a stronger adversary assumes the persona of the double in the eyes of an adept and if this adept, instead of turning away, allows himself to be haunted by that presence. Existence is then structured around this identification and other identifications that are added to it, characterized by an impulse that tends toward excess.

Tesshu is an example of this type. Beginning with a decisive encounter, he experienced permanently the presence of the double, the adversarial master, as he was in the process of struggling against him.

In the case of Musashi, we find the same structure, but the basis of the identification is different. The persona of the double was formed through the combat encounters that he won. Yet the outcome of these encounters remained uncertain right to the end. The vanquished adversary is also the master. The persona of the double associated with past enemies turned into the persona of the adversary yet to be encountered. Musashi oriented himself in relation to this omnipresent enemy, but noted that his equilibrium was maintained by the permanence of his technical and strategic preparation.

The life kata then incorporates partial katas, but the life kata is not just the simple sum of the collection of partial katas, because the intensive practice of katas in an art does not mean that the same structure of mind will dominate the whole of our life. If katas insure the effectiveness of each art, a life kata aims at a particular effectiveness in the life of an individual. Persecuted by the persona of the double, the individual struggles with the techniques of his art, which are extended to become techniques of his life.

By intentionally limiting the field of experience, we allow the state of awareness to take on continually increased intensity and range. Far from being a limitation, the life kata is the vehicle for an effective existential dynamic, as we see in Musashi's mastery of a range of traditional arts.

In Sakoku Japan, the life kata had a social impact because its structure corresponded to that of society as a whole. Moving more deeply along this path led directly to the way in which life was understood socially. For Musashi, making progress on his path and being recognized as a master also implied entering into the service of a feudal lord at the highest level. Yet the disturbing character of his personality several times prevented him from obtaining the high position that he had a right to expect in peaceful Sakoku times.

By contrast, Tesshu enjoyed a very secure social position. The accomplishment of his life kata had brought him general respect, and, at the same time, his connection to his students contributed to his progress along his life kata. For Tesshu, his expertise extended to other traditional arts.

What is the situation today? During the first two years of my stay in France, I trained in karate seven or eight hours a day, and in the evening, exhausted from such intense effort, my body felt as heavy as lead. In this state of fatigue, the movement of my logical intelligence slowed down, but a certain intuitive sensitivity was sharpened. During this period, I think I also experienced a confrontation with the persona of the master—one that haunted me every day. Gradually, I became aware that this constant drive on my part gave rise to a critical attitude in my more educated students. I might even say it was a scorn tinged with fear. At that time, I began my day with one thousand strikes with my right fist, then one thousand with my left fist on a *makiwara* (a moveable plank encased in straw padding). Following this, I made seven hundred to nine hundred strikes with my feet against a training bag.

I wondered about the reasons for this scorn, and I realized that I was harboring an implicit expectation of admiration for the hard and sustained effort I was making. Then I became aware that in Japan I had never encountered this type of attitude; on the contrary, sustained, repetitive efforts were admired.

This traditional attitude about how we should act has survived in Japan and has structured the way a whole generation of salaried employees now work.

PART FOUR

Persistence and Transformation in a Traditional Culture

At the time of my arrival in France in 1971, my image of an ideal man was very much that of a man from Japan's classic era. Such a man discovers his path by deepening his pursuit of an art. His inner strength is to be seen in how he walks and how he is. You see this strength without a need to hear him speak. The practice of martial arts for me was a means of moving forward on this path, but I noticed a disparity between this and how life is lived in France, where an individual must speak and express himself with an exuberance that at first seemed to me to be theatrical. In the French context, my ideal persona—silent and rarely smiling—seemed unpleasant or even ridiculous.

As I began to question why this disparity existed, the importance of implicit communication in Japan and the uniformity that it required became a kind of evidence for me. Although often masked by the modernization and opening of contemporary Japanese society, the forms of sociability established in the closed world of the Edo period were in fact at the foundation of this ideal.

Japanese warriors lived through a time when death—their own as well as the death of others—had become more real, because death seemed to be the extension of familiar movement sequences that they had been learning. For humans, there is something profoundly illogical about death. A society that integrates the idea of death into daily life tends to develop a culture in which intuitive and nonverbal aspects outweigh rationality or the establishment of logical systems. The very real presence of death for the Japanese warrior seems to explain in depth certain characteristics of feudal society, and, on the other hand, it sheds light on the way Japanese society has integrated rationality and Western techniques.

It seems that the structure of the kata, which is very much present at various levels of the collective Japanese psyche, is one of the keys that can help us understand certain traits of that psyche. This, in turn, sheds light on an apparent paradox in Japanese society: the enduring persistence of traditional behavior side by side with an ability to integrate rapid change and to engage in piercing self-criticism.

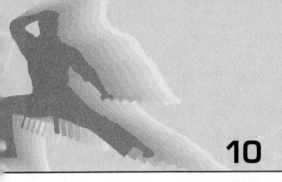

10

SEPPUKU

The Cornerstone of the Warrior's Kata

A key phrase in the education of a warrior's son is: "Because you come from a warrior family, you must be able to carry out seppuku." Seppuku, the kata through which an individual intentionally brings death upon himself, is the exact form with which these children were taught to internalize death as well as life. It is at the center of the formation of the *I* and must be accepted as a prerequisite of social and personal education.

Seppuku is also a societal image that takes on an ambivalence from the harshness of paternal education. This seppuku is the supreme purification that washes away every fault. It is an act of exorcism of the most violent kind, and it is one of the most painful ways to die. Seppuku is spectacular because it distills the whole process of the denial of personal desires into a series of movements that inexorably put an end to life. The more or less prescribed form of these movements is essential in order for seppuku to erase any fault and reintegrate the individual into the group.

Based on factual events, two short stories of Mori Ogai (1862–1922), one of the most influential intellectuals of his time, give a clear picture of seppuku. Mori Ogai was born into a warrior family in which he received a traditional education, but at the same time, he was one of the first Japanese to be steeped in Western culture. Two striking events of the Meiji era (1868–1912)—the Meiji emperor's death and the death by seppuku of General Nogi—profoundly disturbed Mori Ogai and several of his contemporaries.

The Meiji era, which lasted forty-five years, was actually a period of modernization and scientific progress based on the Western model. Following on the heels of the emperor's death, the traditional method of suicide used by one of the leading figures of the country catapulted Japan's traditional values back to the surface.

It was at this time that Mori Ogai wrote a short story, *The Empty Chariot,* which seems to embody his primary concerns at the time. He describes an enormous empty chariot that he encountered numerous times. This chariot is drawn by a sturdy horse that is led by a tall, strong man who strides forward with no regard for anything in his path.

"When they encounter this chariot, those on foot avoid it, horsemen avoid it, the chariots of noblemen avoid it, the cars of the wealthy avoid it, columns of soldiers avoid it, even funeral processions avoid it.

"When he crosses the tracks of the tram, the conductor has to stop the tram so that the chariot can pass. And this chariot is only an empty chariot."

"Each time I encounter this chariot," Mori Ogai writes, "I can't help feeling a touching respect. It goes without saying that I don't intend to compare this empty chariot to a chariot full of objects, even if the objects were extremely precious."

For me, this image stands for the form—that is, the kata—that is passing away. Its meaning comes not from its content, but instead derives from the fact that the man moves forward with a clearly determined form. This image symbolizes the situation of Mori Ogai in relation to Japanese culture and society.

In the years between 1910 and 1920, the Japanese found themselves confronting a transformation of their societal model as they confronted a Western society that was brought to them through socialist ideas and then through the Russian Revolution. During this period, Mori Ogai's choice of literary themes drawn from Japanese history shows that he was turning to his heritage. His traditional education allowed him to internalize the inner structure of a life kata. Yet after he delved very deeply into his discovery of the Western world, his intellectual acuity drove him to see the disparity between his inner world and the social changes to which he had significantly contributed. General Nogi's suicide caused the feeling of this disparity to burst forth, and it was expressed in the form of a kata. Questioning Ogai's personal journey took the radical form of breaking a kata. Faced with the question of his own identity, he sought a response by drawing from Japan's history the tradition that he carried in himself.

TWO HISTORICAL EXAMPLES

The House of the Abe Family tells us how the death in 1641 of Hosokawa Tadatoshi, feudal lord of Higo (known today as Kumamoto), on the island of Kyushu, led to a wave of suicides among those of his vassals who enjoyed his special protection or affection. Using the example of two among them, the author makes clear seppuku's importance and the key role it played.

Upon the death of a feudal lord, suicide was governed by a rule. An individual could not choose suicide on his own. In order to accompany the lord to the other world, it was essential to have his permission, without which the suicide would lose its whole meaning. Tadatoshi bestowed this permission on eighteen vassals who enjoyed his confidence.

One of these, Chojuro, was just a young vassal whose drinking had led him to make a few mistakes. Nevertheless, the protection and good will that Tadatoshi had always shown him meant that he was quite naturally totally devoted to his lord. Upon the death of his master, only one course of action was open to Chojuro: suicide. To survive after the death of his lord would in fact have exposed him to the deepest scorn.

A month later, with no fear of death, he went to his mother's home to inform her of his decision and to bid her farewell. Chojuro, his mother, his wife, and his young brother sat down together and, according to the farewell custom, drank sake together, one after the other, from the same cup. Then, accompanied by his second, he went to Tokoïn Temple to perform his seppuku.

Another figure, Abe Yaichiemon, was a very zealous vassal and a great warrior, impeccable on all counts. Yet Tadatoshi didn't like him much and displayed toward him a dislike that bordered on hatred—feelings that in fact intensified as the years went by. Recently, each time Yaichiemon asked permission to put an end to his days, he was met with a refusal on the part of his lord, who asked him to help his son and successor, Mitsuhisa. Abe therefore had to resolve himself to the dishonor of continuing to live after his lord's death. Talk began to swirl around all this, bringing into question his courage in the face of death. Not being able to withstand these insinuations, he called together his five sons, all of whom were also brave warriors, to be present at his demise. He cut open his gut and slit his throat.

His sons, aware of the affront that this gesture meant for Mitsuhisa, chose to remain united in the face of Mitsuhisa's wrath. Mitsuhisa wasted little time in responding: contrary to the prescription of tradition, the eldest son was deprived of his inheritance, and the fiefdoms were divided into five parts and assigned to each of the descendants, significantly weakening the family.

Gonbei, the eldest, was unable to withstand this humiliation, and a year after the death of Tadatoshi, during a commemorative ceremony, he cut off his topknot and placed it on the altar, indicating thereby his desire to leave the warrior class and become a monk. He was immediately arrested and hanged a few days later for a crime against the spirit of his former lord. His four brothers did not contest his death sentence, but they considered this form of execution unworthy of their brother. In their view, he ought to have been allowed to commit suicide as a warrior instead of dying like a common thief. They and their families took refuge in Gonbei's home, and faced with this new insult, Mitsuhisa condemned them to death. After a final celebratory meal, the women and old men took their lives, the children were dispatched by the sword, and all were buried in the garden. The only ones remaining were those who wanted to fight. All of them perished in the battle waged by the warriors sent by Mitsuhisa and led by an intimate friend of the Abe family.

These two tales remind us that the main reasons that led a warrior to commit seppuku were: to accompany his lord's death (if authorization had been given to do so), carrying out a sanction imposed by his lord, or to repair a fault. When, in the eyes of his lord, a warrior deserved to die, seppuku was the most honorable form of death, because in a way it canceled out the condemnation, unlike the dishonor of execution. *The House of the Abe Family* helps us better understand specific feudal relationships in Japan.

The lord's decision brooked no discussion, and it was only fear or reluctance on the part of the vassals who faced death that could be open to criticism. This story illustrates the societal logic of the Edo era, which aimed to stabilize and maintain the power of the family of the Tokugawa shoguns. Their power resided with the collection of independent and circumscribed fiefdoms, which were directly attached to the shogun who kept them on a very tight leash. In each fiefdom, the value system similarly contributed to maintaining the reigning family, and loyalty to that family was the prime value for each of the vassals. This loyalty was closely linked to the ancestor cult and went back to ancient ties that were perpetuated with exceptional force. This meant that the life or death of vassals amounted to very little compared to loyalty and honor in relation to the family. Further, this determined the central importance assigned to seppuku and the high regard for asceticism and self-sacrifice in the warrior's education.

This history of the Abe family lies at the beginning of the Edo period, but later on, a gap developed between the warriors at the summit of the hierarchy, who departed more and more from this ideal, and the warriors at the bottom of the hierarchy, who were significantly impoverished and clung even more strongly to the values of their class and their education.

Another short story of Mori Ogai, also inspired by real events, shows how warrior values penetrated other layers of the society. *The Sakai Affair* takes place at a time when Westerners exerted intense pressure on Japan. During this troubled period, warriors found themselves facing crucial choices, and, unlike in the previous, less troubled era, numerous seppuku took place.

In January 1868, a conflict developed between the shogun and the emperor, and war broke out in Kyoto. The shogun fled to Edo, but the region around Kyoto and Osaka was beset by a period of uncertainty, and the town of Sakai, an important commercial port, fell under the control of the ancient feudal lords of Tossa.

On February 15, 1868, the Sakai police were informed, though not officially, of the arrival of a ship belonging to the French navy. Because protocol had not been followed, the police decided to forbid the French to enter the city. Yet once evening came, the sailors left their ship, frightening the population with their crude behavior and lack of respect. A violent clash erupted with the Japanese soldiers during which thirteen French sailors were killed.

Three days later, the French consul, Léon Roche, left the ship and demanded a triple reparation: the feudal lord responsible for this affair was to come in person aboard the French ship *Vénus* to apologize; among those who had fired on the French, twenty soldiers, including two captains, were to be executed within three days; and finally, the feudal lord responsible was to pay fifty thousand dollars indemnity to the families of the sailors killed.

The three conditions were accepted. The two captains and two other officers considered themselves to be responsible. All that remained was to designate sixteen soldiers, which was done by drawing lots. All the condemned soldiers then made a significant decision: they accepted death, but only through seppuku in order to avoid dishonor and to become warriors—at the end of the feudal era, soldiers were recruited from several classes, and the warriors filled officer positions in the army. The feudal administration assented to these requests.

The next day, the soldiers dressed in warrior attire and had themselves served a meal with sake. Then, in sedan chairs (*kago*) they traveled to the temple, where they awaited the ceremony as they exchanged pleasantries.

The seppuku site was a square surrounded by canvas that bore the coat of arms of the fiefdoms involved. A member of the imperial family, feudal lords, dignitaries, and the French delegation took their places along three sides, and the remaining side was reserved for the ceremony.

When an officer called the first soldier, Minoura Inokichi, a deep silence fell in the temple. Dressed in the ceremonial costume of a warrior, he sat down. Baba, who was there to decapitate him, stood behind him. Minoura bowed to the lords, and seized the small sword that was presented to him on a platter. He took off his clothing to the level of his belt, drove the sword deeply into his left side, cut downward, then to the right and finally upward several inches. He put down his sword and, staring at the French, pulled out his intestines. Baba managed to behead him only with a third blow.

After Minoura, ten other soldiers also committed seppuku, one after the other. When the turn of the eleventh soldier came, the French consul, very affected by what he had witnessed, exchanged a few words with his sailors, who were also quite agitated, after which they all rose and left without a word. With the French no longer there, the ceremony was halted.

A delegation went to the *Vénus* to meet with the consul. They returned to inform the feudal lords that the consul had been impressed by the self-sacrificial will of the soldiers, that he was unable to withstand more of the gruesome ceremony, and that he requested a pardon for the remaining soldiers on the part of the Japanese state.

The state accepted this request, and nine soldiers were officially received into the warrior class. According to custom, the eleven others were buried as warriors.

SEPPUKU

Death by seppuku is not an easy suicide. What sets it apart is that it demands a strength of will that can endure for a certain time. It is not like jumping off a cliff or like pulling the trigger on a revolver or like swallowing sleeping pills. First of all, the sword blade must be driven into the stomach, and then it must be moved to cut through the abdominal wall so that a part of the intestine falls out of the incision. The individual will sometimes go to the extent of pulling out his intestines.

By convention, seppuku stops there, and an assistant, who has taken up a position behind the victim, decapitates him with a sword blow. If the victim has no assistant, the individual often cuts the carotid artery in his neck to shorten the agony. The act of seppuku requires enormous determination, and it is hard to imagine that it could be carried out fully under the influence of only a sudden or a random impulse. In order to succeed in seppuku, an individual must have not only great physical strength, but also the willpower to withstand fearsome pain during the whole time he plummets toward death.

Seppuku is primarily and fundamentally a social act by means of which the dying person intensely integrates the group supporting him into his act. In fact, his friends and relatives contribute to the serenity of the ceremony.

The House of the Abe Family shows very clearly how eighteen vassals were led to seppuku by the climate, which surrounds the Hosokawa fiefdom, and which plays a decisive and deadly role in Abe's decision. In the successive suicides following the feudal lord's death, the idea is to rejoin him in death, but it is also a choice that elevates the family's standing.

When a warrior receives an order for seppuku as a penalty, he takes it as a mark of respect, because his superior is giving him the chance to prove his quality as a warrior. It is essential, therefore, that he accomplishes seppuku magnificently, because he is reintegrating the group who will honor him as an ancestor. By contrast, execution is a humiliating penalty. That is why, in the Abe family, the four brothers decide to fight the feudal lord after their elder brother has been hanged. Their extermination and the perfect form that they give to their death allows the family honor to be cleansed and allows them to disappear while safeguarding the most durable values. In so doing, they merged with the ideal of the warrior and become exemplary in the memory of the group, which, had they been dishonored, would have disowned them.

In an even more clear-cut way, seppuku gives the Sakai soldiers access to the warrior class.

Seppuku is the kata by means of which, through meeting death, the circle of existence is completed. An individual rises to perfection and excellence through the supreme move of putting an end to his life, while at that very moment he assumes an irreproachable place in the universe. By eradicating his ambivalence, he merges with the multiple representations of the double into which the ancestors, the father, the feudal lord, the master, and the adversary converge. He is drawn to these idealized images, finds himself under their watchful eye, and battles with them his whole life.

In the earliest known documents, dating from the eighth century, we already find a form of seppuku. With the warriors' ascension to power, examples become more numerous and take on a legendary character.

During the Warring States period (fifteenth to sixteenth centuries), Japan underwent a century of warfare, and cases of seppuku were very numerous. At a time when combat techniques were being perfected, the attitude of the warriors with regard to death settled into an esthetic formalization of death, which then found expression in two models: combat and seppuku.

The choice of the stomach (*hara*) comes from a mythological belief that locates the seat of the soul in this spot. Feeling, courage, and strength are also to be found there, so it is considered the center of the body—or, rather, the center of a life. In all the martial arts, through working with the breath and concentration, we learn to place our energy and to feel our strength at the level of the hara, the lower stomach. Speaking with real sincerity is "to speak with an open stomach." The act of seppuku is linked directly to this concept of the body. Opening the stomach allows an individual to prove, through his courage and strength, his decisive sincerity.

The Sakai Affair throws light on the disparity between the French and the Japanese of that time in how death was viewed. The French consul demands the execution of twenty soldiers, but the soldiers request death by seppuku. For the consul, the execution means nothing more than a volley of bullets, which in a way shortens the process of death and encases it in an abstract form; the weight of death is avoided through the speed of the bullets.

In our day, this tendency toward abstraction generally dominates the relationship that modern society has with death: the individual is very insensitive to death, which is distanced from everyday life. As soon as it comes close to us, we no longer know how to understand it, we are crushed, and we demand that society release us from it quickly.

The attitude of the nineteenth-century French toward seppuku is the general attitude in today's world. Japan is no exception and does its best to hide this earlier attitude toward death. The descriptions of seppuku in the short stories of Mori Ogai shock all postwar Japanese, and the seppuku of the writer Mishima in 1970 had a stronger impact because it propelled to the surface a past that was still uncomfortably close.

11

THE WARRIOR'S KATA IN CONTEMPORARY SOCIETY

In 1970, Yukio Mishima's suicide was a real shock for me and for the students of my generation. For us, caught as we were in a double culture, this act amounted to a breaking point, and somehow I never stopped wondering about it. Through understanding the concept of kata, though, I think that I understand it much better now.

By means of his acuity as a man of letters, Mishima highlighted the problem of identity and conflict, which, although often blocked and most often buried in the unconscious, arises forcefully for the Japanese. That is why reactions to his suicide were extremely violent. Most people explained it as an act of madness, the result of a sudden crisis, or as a surface feature of his personality. The violence of this rejection of his act was a kind of self-protection—a burying, once again, of the questions of identity that this seppuku had brought to the surface.

Mishima was one of the authors who most influenced young Japanese intellectuals through his literary work of the 1950s and through his socio-political speeches on existential action during the 1960s. When I was a student in Tokyo from 1967 to 1971, I was very aware of his speeches and his spectacular activities. His warlike exhibitionism (disguising himself as a samurai, stints in the army, exhibitions of photos of himself in the role of St. Sebastian, the creation of a personal militia one hundred strong) seemed anachronistic to us and sometimes made us snigger. Yet for those of my generation who were looking for a meaning to life, a Mishima stage was inevitable. For Mishima, who was twenty years older than I, the brutal transformation of values that he experienced at the end of the war was something we were living through in the gap we felt between ourselves and our parents.

As I grew to be the age of the *kamikaze* (suicide) pilots, my world was turned upside-down. Twenty years separated me from them. At my age they went to their deaths, and for me and my fellow young people, it was inconceivable to think of deliberately moving toward death. What did we face that could justify taking our own lives?

Before he committed the act, Mishima had explicitly shown how attracted he was to this way of dying. On stage or on camera, he had several times played the role of a character who died by seppuku. Like all those of his generation, he could not forget that he had grown up during the war, a time when young men were prepared to die at the age of twenty.

His speeches struck us with the radicalism of an action that always led toward death. In my generation's experience, taking action and death were poles apart. After the war, education had adopted the opposite view from the preceding generation, and we felt the disparity between the values that filtered through from our parents and those we were taught at school.

MISHIMA AND THE *HAGAKURE*

Dating from the beginning of the eighteenth century, the *Hagakure* is a treatise written for warriors on the art of living and the art of dying. During World War II, it was considered a sacred book of dying. It was widely disseminated throughout all of Japan, and it was used to impart a value system to the soldiers. Because it dealt mainly with the attitude of warriors who faced death, the book was criticized right after the war and was thought to have actually been one of the sources of military fanaticism.

In 1967, Mishima wrote an *Initiation to the Hagakure*. These few paragraphs of introduction are illustrative of his conception of taking action and of death:

I have only one book now—*Hagakure* by Yamamoto Jocho. I began reading it during the war. For more than twenty years now, I have always kept it near my desk. I reread it often, and each time it makes a very deep impression on me. It seems to be the only book of its kind for me.

Hagakure began to shine in me once we came to the end of wartime, when it had been popular and had in fact been required reading. Perhaps *Hagakure* has always been a paradoxical book. During the war, *Hagakure* was a luminous body in the light, but it is in darkness that it truly shines.

Shortly after the war, I began my writing career.

At that time, there burgeoned around me a new era and a new literature. But I felt no sympathy at all—either ideological or artistic—for postwar literature.

The energy and vitality of those who had other ideological experiences and other literary sensibilities brushed by me and petered out, like hurricanes.

Of course I felt my isolation and thought deeply about it, searching for what there was in me of the last remaining coherent foundation from wartime and the postwar period. . . .

At the same time, there was a need for this coherent book that had sustained me to immediately approve of my unique upbringing. It had to sustain solidly all aspects of my isolated position, which was contrary to the times. And this book had to be rejected by the era. *Hagakure* met every one of these requirements.[1]

Hagakure—or, more precisely, *Hagakure Monjo* (literally, *monjo,* "written from what has been heard"; *hagakure,* "hidden among the leaves")—relates conversations of Yamamoto Jocho and Tashiro Tsuramoto, who faithfully transcribed them. Yamamoto Jocho (1659–1719) was a warrior from a fiefdom in the south of Japan. His feudal lord died in 1700 without authorizing him to commit seppuku in order to follow him. Yamamoto then gave up his status as a warrior and became a hermit monk. Ten years later, Tashiro Tsuramoto, a vassal from the same fiefdom, paid him a visit. Their conversations, which took place over a period of seven years, are recorded in the *Hagakure.* The book began to circulate among the warriors of the fiefdom and became a kind of code of moral conduct for them.

Mishima found his life's guiding light in *Hagakure.* Here are two extracts from it:

I have understood that the essential element of the way of the warrior (bushidō) is to die. When it is a question of living or dying, it is better to die without hesitation. There are no complicated reasons. Just go forward with determination. In the calculating bushidō of Kamigata,* dying before achieving one's aim is a useless death. It is clear that we would rather live than die. So it is natural to find reasons for living. But if you choose to live without succeeding, that is cowardice. That is the difficulty. On the other hand, if you choose death, even if you are criticized by those who say that it is a useless death or madness, it is not shameful. That is the essential element of the way of the warrior. Morning and night, you need to face the decision to die. By integrating this decision into your existence, you will acquire bushidō, and you will be carrying out your duty perfectly, faultlessly, through the whole of your life. . . .

Every day, you must renew the thought of death. You must quiet the body and the mind every morning, and think how to die,

---

*Kamigata was the region of Osaka where trade was very developed. Jacho Yamamoto says that mercantile thinking can be seen in the warrior mind-set in this region.

whether from an arrow, a gun, a spear, or a sword, whether you are engulfed by the waves, whether you fall into a great fire, whether you are hit by lightning or by an earthquake, whether you fall off a cliff, or even die from illness or accident. In thinking of the end of your life, you must place yourself in death every morning without hesitation. A sage of yesteryear said, "When leaving a house, you must be among the dead; passing the threshold, you go forward to meet enemies." This saying is not about caution; it is about the attitude that allows you to outdistance death.

In *The Psychology of the Japanese* (1953), Minami Hiroshi severely criticizes *Hagakure,* which he considers to be a breviary of death-centered fanaticism. Because the author is especially sensitive to the "air"* of the times, his book is indicative of the dominant tendencies in intellectual circles in postwar Japan, when the country was engaged in reconstruction. Minami Hiroshi's harsh criticism of traditional culture was in reaction to his own experience during the war, a period in which the predominance of that culture reached its peak and was an extension of the return to traditional values that had begun in the 1930s.

This critical current was very far-reaching; it went so far as to discuss methods for the complete Westernization of Japan, including a revamping of the language. In 1946, Shiga Naoya, a famous writer of the prewar period, even proposed the following complete language reform: "I think it would be good on this occasion for us to adopt the best and the most beautiful language in the world. I think that the French language most suits these qualifications. . . ." This quotation sets the tone for the proposition that he develops in the magazine *Kaizo* (Reorganization) on the topic of the problem of the national language.

In much the same way, right after the Meiji Restoration, there was a strong tendency to undervalue Japanese culture and to attempt to substitute Western culture in its place. Minami Hiroshi observes that

---

*See more on this term in the section Air (*Kuki*) and the Non-said, in chapter 12.

obedience was imposed by force on the Japanese, and he shows that the forced docility of military life was a historical creation: "This kind of general spirit of obedience creates an automatic habit of submission to authority, and prevents a free development of the ego. Or, to put it another way, by blocking development of the ego, the habit of obedience is reinforced.

"It's best to let yourself be carried by the main current. This attitude is coupled with the teaching of *non-I* from former times. Moral texts for general use by the population of the Edo period constantly insist on this *non-I*. . . . Among the warriors, a spirit of loyalty developed that negated the *I*."[2]

Paradoxically for Minami, by affirming the notion of "You must live by doing what you want to do," the *Hagakure* includes a teaching of egoism. I will come back to this point by comparing his interpretation with that of Mishima.

In analyzing the Japanese concept of the fragility of happiness, based on the Buddhist idea of evanescence, Minami puts forward the notion of nihilism, which he defines in the following way. "It means forming a mental attitude which, in whatever situation, keeps us from sinking into sadness because we know that life is full of changes. It means taking evanescence as a negative kind of mental immunization against misfortune. This is the attitude that warriors and soldiers have toward death. . . .

"The idea of evanescence forms two sides of the same shield: one is immunization against misfortune, and the other is the expectation of happiness. . . ."[3]

Where Minami sees a downward spiral toward resignation, Mishima finds a guiding beacon for his life. For Mishima, the statement, "I have understood that the essence of bushidō is to die" is "a paradox that symbolizes the whole of this book":

In being repressed, the explosive power of the death wish moves inward and reaches its maximum intensity and danger. Bringing death to the surface of awareness is an important element for the health of mind and spirit, and yet it is completely ignored. . . . Having death in your thoughts every day is the same as having life in your thoughts every day. The *Hagakure* is insistent about this.[4]

By contrast, for Minami, the thought of death in the *Hagakure* is a "tendency to always expect the worst."

It is a very Japanese attitude to give up in advance. . . . Therefore, having the probability of death in mind in order to avoid an act of cowardice is neither caution, nor is it being forewarned—it is a passive and negative psychological attitude. . . . Misfortune as a psychological solution is pushed . . . to such an extent that positive enjoyment is derived from a state of dissatisfaction. This is close to a masochism that derives enjoyment from self-harassment; it is a psychological trait that could be called "Japanese masochism."[5]

In conclusion, Minami considers that the *Hagakure* teaches a technique that allows warriors to live better in submission within a closed system.

Opposing this point of view, in his *Initiation to the Hagakure,* Mishima asserts that this book "speaks of liberty and passion."

I have found in this book my most important reason for living. . . .

Art withers as soon as it is no longer threatened and as soon as it no longer receives encouragement from something other than art itself. For art, life is both mother and enemy. Life is within the artist and constitutes an eternal antithesis for art. Over a long period, I found a philosophy of life in *Hagakure*. . . . Its influence made my life as an artist abnormally difficult, but at the same time, it was my matrix for literature and an eternal source of vitality through its merciless demands, through its critique, through its severity, and through its icy beauty. . . .

It is normal that man's vital instinct latches onto life when it is a question of either life or death. But when a man wants to live and die in a beautiful way, he must realize that his attachment to life continually betrays life's beauty. Death elevates the striving and the purity of love. This is the ideal of love that *Hagakure* teaches.[6]

Becoming aware of death seemed salutary to him: "In being repressed, the explosive power of the death wish moves inward and reaches its maximum intensity and danger. Bringing death to the surface of awareness is an important element for the health of the mind and spirit, and yet it is completely ignored . . . . Having death in your thoughts every day is the same as having life in your thoughts every day." For Mishima, this is the second stage of *Hagakure*'s teaching, and is found in the following passage: "Man's life is short. You must live while doing what you want to do. It is stupid to live disagreeably, doing things you don't like. But this idea is a secret that I've never been able to speak to young people for fear that they would distort it, not having understood it properly. For example, in my current situation I may like to sleep, but would I then live my life sleeping and not go out?"[7]

Mishima sees in this text a "philosophy with two sides, like a shield carrying both life and death." On the contrary, this "astonishing" passage seems to Minami to indicate an egoism engendered by resistance to the requirement of submission during the feudal era, a tendency that became amplified later: "After the Meiji era, oppression by the state and submission to the state continued, and resistance appeared not in the form of a negation of authority, but most often as an egocentricity mixed with egoism."[8]

For Minami, this derives from the fact that the Japanese conquered the awareness of the ego not by overthrowing the authority that had imposed negation on them, but instead, that authority was overthrown by a foreign power. What grew out of this was a mistrust of authority that expanded to a total mistrust of humankind so that, being able to have confidence only in himself, each individual's self-interest became paramount.

In the philosophy of *Hagakure,* Mishima sees a freedom revealed that is to be found by always maintaining an impulse toward death. This freedom inspires in him a concept of taking action that leads him to seppuku:

Leading up to the judgment of a situation that engenders the decision to die is a long chain of earlier judgments. Continual training in determination includes moments of extended stress and concentration that a man of action must withstand.

The world of a man of action is like a ring that he outlines in his mind and that must end in a closing point. Each time, he rejects the ring, which, lacking a final point, is not closed, and he goes on to another ring—and so on, one after the other.

The world of the artist or the philosopher is made up of increasingly larger concentric circles. But when death approaches, which circle will have the greatest feeling of achievement?

The death that finishes off one's world at the very moment that the final point is placed—will not such a death include a much stronger feeling of completeness?

The greatest misfortune for a man of action is not meeting death after having set down this impeccable point. . . . *Hagakure's* lesson on death indicates not the result of taking action but the true happiness for a man of action. Nasu No Yoichi lived for a long time after his arrow pierced the fan. . . .*

---

*In the twelfth century, during a decisive battle, one of the sides withdrew to its ships at sea. A ship approached, rocked by heavy waves, with an elegant lady aboard accompanied by her retinue. She sang out a challenge, inviting an archer to shoot at a fan attached to an upright pole fixed to the ship. It was an extremely difficult shot because of the rough seas. Nasu No Yoichi, who had been chosen to meet the challenge, advanced a few feet into the sea on horseback and shot. His success was honored by both sides.

THE CONTRADICTORY SEARCH
FOR A LIFE KATA

In writing his praise of the *Hagakure,* Mishima turned toward an action that, to use his words, "closed an unfinished ring by placing its final point."

From his youth on, he structured his approach to literature on the model of identifications of kata. "I identified with Radiguet's image,* because I too should have died at twenty. . . . By making Radiguet my rival, I used his novel as a goal that I had to move beyond. . . ." His technique of the short story (that of Akinari), like an artfully polished crystal, had grown in me as the ideal form for the Japanese novel.

The structure of the identifications tended toward that of a kata because of the closeness of death, which imposed a limitation on him and led him to narrow his ideal image in a precise way. In so doing, the persona of Radiguet allowed him to merge into one the master, rival, and death.

Unlike traditional arts, however, the blending did not have a technical structure that included the body, which meant it was not really a kata. Indeed, the katas of traditional arts, even though not always obvious to a Westerner, always include a technique that brings the whole body into play—its rhythm, its postures, its breathing—in short, a regulated way of working.

Ten years before his death, Mishima wrote a short novel, *Yukoku* (Patriotism), based on a historical event. In 1936, after the failure of a coup d'état, a lieutenant committed suicide by seppuku. At the core of this story, Mishima outlines the relationship between the lieutenant and his wife—for Mishima, love and death were intimately connected. The lieutenant committed suicide after making love.

Five years later, Mishima adapted this story into a movie in which he played the role of the lieutenant. In this film, he sees himself hav-

---

*[Raymond Radiguet (1903–1923), a French author that met an untimely death at age twenty. —*Ed.*]

ing the body he imagined and projected. His own body becomes superimposed and identifies with the bodies that had been the object of his love in the preceding years (see *Confessions of a Mask*).[9] Later, after his suicide, anyone who had seen his film was struck by its similarities.

The lieutenant incarnated the values of loyalty and faithfulness to the emperor and located himself within a military kata linked to tradition, but which, by Mishima's day, was outmoded. It is clear that Mishima actually tried to forge a kata through the practice of martial arts, but, as the case of Tesshu shows, the process of including the structure of our life in the kata of martial arts is long and difficult. The building of the complex persona of the double (who is both the master and the adversary) is the product of intense work for an entire life. This building happens through the practice of martial arts techniques. It must be said that Mishima entered this path very late in his life and, in spite of the regularity of his two weekly training periods and the intensity of his effort, he was unable to bridge the gap. He was obliged then arbitrarily to choose an adversary. "For me, action is the starting point. I think that I am among those who deeply sense that one's thought and one's spirit weaken in the absence of an enemy. . . . Therefore, I absolutely need an enemy. I chose the Communist Party . . . whose theory is completely incompatible with the idea of a ruling emperor. The emperor is the unique and precious symbol of our historical continuity, cultural integrity, and ethnic identity."

The wavering and divided nature of contemporary society obliged him arbitrarily to fabricate a loyalty that would have been taken for granted in a traditional setting. The martial arts kata on which he would have liked to structure his life, following the *Hagakure,* did not have the necessary breadth, and, in addition, bringing this into alignment with his literary activities was impossible.

In spite of all this, Mishima's intention was pulled in the direction of a life kata as outlined by *Hagakure:* "If a man gives himself the moral aim of living continuously in this way, and if he places the ultimate criterion of this beauty in death, each day will be imbued with continual striving."

With disdain for a relaxed life, the *Hagakure* advocates a rationale for living in flawless striving every day. This means a battle in daily life—and such is the life of a warrior. For a man who is attracted to this kind of kata but who does not possess the necessary technical structure of the kata, there is no better way of attaining it than through a complete and instantaneous identification with a figure from the past. And so, Mishima became identified with the image of the lieutenant from *Yukoku,* brought to life in his film, and later, as we shall see, with Yoshida Shoin, a figure from the end of the Edo period. *Hagakure* led Mishima to enter into the life kata of a warrior who, in his movement toward death, allowed Mishima to consummate a profound striving.

Hagakure is based on the reality of the practice of martial arts, which means a body disciplined by the lengthy work of katas and training. The more Mishima was trained by *Hagakure,* the more he entered a world where the body was important. Still, he suffered for a long time with a sickly, delicate body—a suffering that was intensified because of his strong homosexual leanings.

At the age of twenty-seven, during a voyage to Greece, he was struck by the beauty of the statues, and his aspiration for physical health was awakened. Upon his return, he wrote *Kinjiki* (Forbidden Sex),[10] which became the first homosexual novel to be published in Japan.

His subsequent book, *The Sound of Waves,* is a hymn to beauty and bodily strength. After publishing this book, Mishima dedicated himself to working on his own body, creating an ideal image in so doing—the image of the body he would have liked to have had. Subsequently, following the structure of the kata, his efforts of identification with this image continued relentlessly in the consistency and regularity of his work on muscle building and martial arts. His life kata was beginning to take shape. For Mishima, his construction of an ideal image preceded his determination in attaining it.

At the age of forty-five, Mishima committed suicide, and we are able to follow the long chain of events that led him to seppuku.

At the age of thirty, he began his physical training. It seems that in the kata of martial arts, his latent homosexuality found an outlet in the structured contacts during training sessions. It also seems that in the complex play of identifications, his sexuality appeared not directly as a homosexual urge, but instead, it was sublimated in the hierarchical distance that separates the master and blends the desire for identification with the multiple personae of the double—that is, the image of perfection. When this desire for identification unfolds at a hierarchical, societal level and facilitates sublimation, the subject wants to possess subtly and become the double—that is to say, a person.

Five years before Mishima's death, the year of the film *Yokoku,* he began writing *The Sea of Fertility,* his last novel. All through this work, we can glimpse his plunge toward death. In his first two books, his language is not yet explicitly oriented toward seppuku.

Three years before his death, he formed a paramilitary militia. According to his writer friend Hojo Makoto, he had a propensity for taking spectacular or even exhibitionist action in any given situation, but from 1968 on, there was a change in this attitude. The more he deepened his kata, the more he consolidated and limited the reach of his literary activities. Several of his friends confirmed this—Mishima's writing changed at this time; in fact, he had difficulty writing at all.

The life kata that was beginning to be forged in him awakened contradictory impulses, because he was forced to create it without having a technical kata that could bring a sufficiently strong structure in relation to the reach of his literary ambitions. In writing *The Sea of Fertility,* he states, "I have devoted all that I have received from life to this novel. When it is finished, I will be completely empty."

He had just published *Initiation to the Hagakure,* in which his attachment to death through taking action is strongly affirmed. "We must admit that the work begins to give forth its living light when we work as if we were to die today."[11] In this book, we can see the evidence of a drive that carries Mishima toward the accomplishment of his kata.

Following the image of a world built as concentric circles, Mishima at this stage added one more circle that drew him closer to his final goal. Only through seppuku would he attain that goal.

MISHIMA'S SEPPUKU

On November 25, 1970, Mishima had an appointment with General Mashita in a military barracks in the heart of Tokyo.[12]

At 10:45, wearing a sword, Mishima arrived for his appointment, accompanied by four disciples who carried concealed knives and ropes. By means of a surprise assault, they overpowered the general and tied him up. With pale and tense faces, they barricaded themselves in the room.

Mishima demanded that the soldiers be assembled on the grounds below the balcony. He draped banners, threw down leaflets and made a speech to the soldiers for about ten minutes. The soldiers had trouble hearing him and interrupted him several times with shouting. Finally, the speech ended with "Long live the emperor!"

Returning to the barricaded room, Mishima declared, "I could not have acted in any other way." He took off his jacket, sat in the traditional position for seppuku, and plunged his sword into his stomach. His disciple Morita, the head of his militia, tried three times to sever Mishima's head, but he failed. His friend Kogu replaced him, and he finally severed Mishima's head.

Taking Mishima's sword, Morita committed seppuku beside Mishima's body, and Kogu cut off Morita's head.

This course of events clearly delineates Mishima's goal: the flawless carrying out of his seppuku. His goal was not a successful coup d'état. The role of each one of the participants in the accomplishment of his seppuku had been meticulously prepared, as in a well-choreographed piece of theater.

As Mishima had said himself, he wanted to die not as a literary figure, but as a warrior. During his time, however, there were no warriors either in the sense of bushi or in the military sense, because, according to the 1946 constitution, Japan did not have an army. A compromise amendment however allowed for the formation of a so-called self-defense force that could not be aligned officially with any militaristic ideology. This armed force, lacking any clear identity, wavered between reminiscences of the past and unsatisfying images offered by the imposed democracy and by American models.

In 1960, the renewal of the Japan-U.S. security treaty, which had placed Japan under the military protection of the United States, gave rise to violent demonstrations. This treaty was scheduled to be renewed ten years later, and in the face of mounting social unrest and an increase in the number of demonstrations, much more forceful protests were expected during 1970. Yet after considerable violence in 1968 and 1969, especially in the universities, the year 1970 turned out to be relatively calm.

No doubt, Mishima was counting on having his lightning blow recorded against the backdrop of a society in turmoil. Even though the planned scenario defaulted on him, the logic of his kata sustained him. Already, in 1969, he had declared many times that he was preparing to die, sword in hand. In addition, reaching the age of forty-five meant that he was almost at a limit beyond which it would be impossible for him to die beautifully in action.

As the year 1970 approached, the multiple personae of the double became clearer and also came closer to that of the warrior. This connects no doubt to the following presentiment: "After having written *The Sea of Fertility*, I am afraid I may find nothing more." This also may explain the change in him that was noticed by his friends.

Yet it would be quite wrong to think that Mishima had thought much about or foreseen his seppuku very far ahead of time. His path toward it was determined along the course of his struggle with the persona of the double whose various faces appeared through sometimes contradictory words and signs. At the time of his seppuku, Mishima wore a headband emblazoned with the words, "Again seven times, live and fight for the motherland." These words were based on the image of a fourteenth-century warrior who died fighting for the emperor. The saying makes references to the Buddhist belief that we reincarnate seven times, a theme that Mishima had used in *The Sea of Fertility.*

The date Mishima chose for his seppuku, November 25, was the anniversary of the death of Yoshida Shoin, who was executed on November 25, 1859, at the age of twenty-nine. Yoshida Shoin was a revolutionary warrior whose activity and ideas had an important impact during the time leading up to the Meiji revolution. Already known for his ideological and philosophical writing, Yoshida boarded an American ship, braving what he knew to be forbidden, in the hopes of being taken to the United States to study. Worried about the reaction of the Japanese government, the Americans refused to take him, and he was arrested.

The choice of circumstances for Mishima's seppuku symbolizes the series of identifications to which he had connected himself.

The various explanations put forward to explain his suicide—a coup d'état, a violent initiative, the dead end in his literary career, his search for an ideological impact in society, his psychological problems, madness—seem incomplete. His progress toward seppuku is better explained by the structure of kata, which assembles these contradictory and entangled elements.

All his military allusions—the militia, the uniform, the harangue, the choice of setting—are the formal constituents of the kata that he had created in order to build, following the *Hagakure,* a persona of the forces with which he was struggling and the images of identification toward which he was striving. As he had declared several times during the course of his last years, only death could bring his acts to a conclusion by closing the incomplete circle, by reconciling irreconcilables.

Mishima created a kata, a weapon with which he struggled and with which he trained. The closer he came to death, the more his life kata became coherent. In this sense, Mishima's suicide was not a failure, but the creation of his kata.

12

EFFECTIVENESS AND WEIGHT OF THE KATAS

THE AIR (*KUKI*) AND THE NON-SAID

In current Japanese usage, *kuki* means both the "air" that we breathe and "ambience" or "atmosphere."

This term indicates an assessment or at least a form of social recognition of facts that emerge from group psychology and that are repressed and thrown back into the unconscious, because rationalization is the collective form on which people rely. These facts exist to a lesser extent in Western societies.

For example, in a large group, to justify voting for something that you had argued against, you might say, "I couldn't do otherwise, because the 'air' of the assembly went in that direction."

Yamamoto Shichihei writes:

An individual feels that his own decision is constrained by an intangible "air." This means that he is won over not by the conclusion that would result from the discussion, which he just led, but by this "air."

A man cannot escape from the air in the sense of kuki any more than he can escape from air in its ordinary sense. Consequently, when he arrives at a conclusion, it is not a logical result; instead it is an adaptation to the air. It is the air that decides yes or no. Because of this, when someone refuses, saying it is the air, we have no way of contradicting him, because we cannot have a discussion with the air. *Air* is a very accurate term to indicate a certain situation. We are certainly constrained by the colorless and transparent air; its existence is definitely hard to pin down. The indefinable, absolute limitation would be spiritual air.[1]

This is how Yamamoto Shichihei describes the strong sensitivity that the Japanese have to the surrounding atmosphere. It often happens that they display behavior that elsewhere would be considered incredibly opportunistic. They seem to let themselves be dominated by the kuki as if it were the vehicle of a tendency that is implicitly convenient to go along with.

We realize that the word seems to have absolute authority in all circumstances and it exerts an astonishing force:

- Such a decision can be criticized, but in the air that reigned at the conference . . .
- If we speak while taking into account the air of the assembly . . .
- If you criticize without knowing the air of the society during that period . . .
- Don't claim that you have thought deeply without being familiar with the air of the place . . .
- The air of the place was completely different from what I expected . . .
- and so forth.[2]

In his book, he reports numerous examples of irrational collective behavior justified by kuki. The explanation that he provides is on the level of existential psychology rather than sociology. According to him, in group situations, the Japanese were much more likely to invest emotionally in a relationship whose object seemed to be more or less a supernatural entity.

The kuki leads a group to unanimous conduct. To a greater or lesser extent, this phenomenon happens everywhere nowadays, especially when there is a crisis (either an economic crisis or an unexpected event). At such times, each person's individuality is completely engulfed in group behavior because of the kuki.

Yamamoto Shichihei bases his thinking on the experience of World War II, during which Japanese society endured an extremely dramatic situation that brought to the surface certain behavior that would have been covered up in times of peace. For him, this behavior has not changed at all in our day, and the drive toward this potentially destructive, irrational way of thinking is still present in Japanese society.

Taking them as extreme cases and connecting them with current examples, he cites several experiences that he lived through during the war. In doing so, he shows himself to be a lucid observer of the behavior of those who are forced to live in daily contact with death.

The *Yamato* was the largest warship in the world during World War II and the last remnant of an already ruined fleet. In his study of the last mission of the *Yamato,* which sank in the Battle of Okinawa, Yamamoto Shichihei recalls that this mission had been judged hopeless by the officers of the central command. He makes use of this example in order to study what leads men to make a decision whose outcome can be nothing other than catastrophic.

The following astonishing statement of Vice-Admiral Osawa Jisaburō, second-in-command of the fleet, appeared as part of an article on the battleship *Yamato* in the magazine *Bungei Shunju,* in August 1975: "I thought and I still think today that the mission of the *Yamato* was completely normal because of the general "air" of those times.

"In studying the documentation, it seems that all those who condemned the mission of the *Yamato* based their arguments on precise analysis showing the recklessness of this strategy. Whereas those who were for the mission had no objective argument to justify it. The basis of their argument was "air." So even in such a serious case, all the discussions were cut short by the 'air.'"

Forming structure through kata and sensitivity to air as described by Yamamoto Shichihei are complementary and originate in the same social reality. As we have seen, the transmission and communication of kata is based on the consensus of a shared experience that is not formulated in words. Moreover, in Japan the dominant forms of social behavior do not allow display of emotion. Instead, "sensibility is educated to decode intonation of the voice, body language, in short, whatever is suggested in a more or less unconscious way."[3]

Spoken language within a group always leaves much latitude to the non-said, which is nevertheless communicated in an implicit way. This fact is often missed by foreigners who, even if they are quite fluent in the Japanese language, are surprised at the reticence of the Japanese to respond to them in Japanese: apparently the non-said cannot operate unless there is an identification with the group.

In the Japanese countryside, neighborhoods are sufficiently scattered so that the language of the group is dominant and the traditional way of speaking is maintained. In the city, the situation is more complex, and it seems that several forms of language intersect. Groups that are more or less limited in size actually constitute units (families, groups of coworkers, or friends), each of which have their own non-said, varying according to the dominant mode of communication within the group. Urban life, however, also requires a quicker, more superficial communication for which we use a more academic language that has a more explicit and logical character.

This diversity in what the speaker takes into account has been implanted into the structure of the Japanese language. Famous haiku* are certainly based on the non-said. They are therefore untranslatable,

---

*Short traditional poems of seventeen syllables in the regulated form of three lines of five syllables, seven syllables, and five syllables.

because the meaning of the words alone does not take into account the sound, rhythm, and especially sensations and images associated with the words.

古池や	*Furuike ya*	Old pond *ya* (exclamation)
蛙飛びこむ	*Kawazu tobikomu*	Frog jumps in
水の音	*Mizu no oto*	Water sound

The sound *furu* (*furui*, "old") evokes for me the color of something old and slightly fuzzy and also the image of my great-grandfather, whom I called Furui-ji-san, and who died at the age of almost one hundred when I was eight. The particularly greenish color of his bones that we collected after the cremation makes me think of a respected old age. *Furuike*, "old pond": This sound—caressing but at the same time dusty—brings to mind the image of an old pond surrounded by woods in which we would play. It is also the old mossy pond near a Zen temple where I often lingered during high school, and it is the calm of its old forest, the antiquity of the temple, and so on. This is how the sound gives rise to a multitude of colored, tactile images.

Ya is an exclamation that, like an arrow let fly, reinforces the statement. This word, which also means "arrow," brings up childhood memories for me.

Kawa is the river, the river of childhood, the taste of water in my mouth. In diving, it is the consistency—sandy or pebbly—of the riverbed and the image of children swimming like frogs.

Kawazu is a literary word for "frog" (we now say *kaeru*). The green color of the water, the word *kawazu*, which I learned in high school, already evokes the image of the dive. These images take shape with the word *tobikomu* (dive).

Tobikomu is the calm of the mountain that is disturbed by the sound of the dive as it breaks the surface of the pond. It is the circles of the dive that gently move out on the green water, breaking against the little rock from which the frog dived in and where, before that, he sat immobile, as if in meditation. The surface, like a translucent film, shows the water's depth, opens for an instant, and then closes.

Mizu no oto, the sound of the water, was already evoked by the preceding word.

This collection of sounds, this music, calms me, almost cradles me. Its rhythm gives a very reassuring impression. I have stopped with the first images that arise, trying to give only an impression. I don't know what English-speaking people can feel when reading the translation, but it seems to me that the non-said—which for me was an experience shared within a village childhood and a way of life—would have to be different in their culture, in their world of forms and colors.

If I made a painting of this haiku, it would depict the old pond of a Zen temple. And I think that the sound, the quality of the words, produces a vision of nature emerging from childhood or adolescence that, for the Japanese, would come together in an image of a water surface, which we could find in paintings that they are likely to make of this haiku.

The sound and the rhythm through which we taste the dimensions, the form, and the touch of words are the communication strength of this haiku. In fact, haiku are a highly developed form of the expression of the non-said.

What is communicated by means of these poems rises up, with force, like an air bubble from the recesses of feeling. When two people communicate using haiku, they understand each other, and the exchange is satisfying. Because people are not used to formulating their feelings explicitly, describing and explaining what they feel seems like a complicated affair, and in the end, it is not very satisfying because understanding loses most of its depth.

Because they are immersed in a shared experience and because they use the imagistic richness of ideograms (kanji), the sounds and words of haiku offer multiple images without having to connect them in sequences. The images are apprehended as in a dream, like a many-petaled flower.

In appreciating a haiku, the mind opens to images buried in memory—such as joy or bitterness from the past, regret, and satisfaction; wellsprings from the unconscious. When a Japanese poet writes, the tip of his brush, soaked in ink, includes all these images; he imbues the words with them, without, however, setting them down on the page.

Haiku is a kata in which the rules and the limited number of words are an elaborate means of expression. The refined form of the haiku is a condensed form of the manifestation of the non-said in Japanese culture—which is why these poems are of interest in our study of kata.

Of course, the non-said is not unique to Japan, but Japanese society has accorded it a prominent niche. Yamamoto Shichihei's study on kuki is, as far as we know, the first work to look into this question.

Among Japanese, a discussion is more like a long series of presentations that cannot be interrupted before each speaker has finished without the interrupter being considered impolite. Each response is also a contribution that unfolds without being interrupted. The logical thread is not woven together in the same way as in an English discussion, in which the sporadic exchange of contradictory propositions is appropriate.

In Japan, then, the way communication takes place demands that reactions to what someone has said do not rise to the surface. In a group, when the non-said is fairly consistent, the reactions are not just held in check; instead, they tend to form the air of the group.

What arises from the realm of the non-said has a rich content and is communicable to those who have acquired the same sensitivity. This way of communicating is hard to grasp, because its signs are veiled and discrete. Nevertheless, it connects with the subconscious and it is immediate.

The weight of the non-said within a group reflects the intensity of identification of its members. When the sociability of the group is based mainly on this identification, it seems that less must be said, channels converge and seem to spring up from the past, and the group is likely to place itself in a kata—one of a class or order as discussed earlier.

FROM THE MEIJI ERA
TO WORLD WAR II

The kata can be defined as a precise, ritualized social model that is transmitted with particular care paid to its exact forms. Its specificity in relation to other cultural models that it might be compared to lies in the rigor of its technical composition and in the psychological structure that it requires.

After the opening of Japan at the end of the nineteenth century, the deployment of katas is what gave Japanese society its strength. Sakoku society generated katas at the cost of a harsh autocracy that could have turned into simple stagnation. By contrast, the process of interiorization that was then set in motion developed a kind of centripetal force, set apart from changes in the outside world but rich in a potential for initiatives.

It would be a mistake to try fitting all the cultural and social models of Japan into the kata mold. The possibility of directing an individual's energy into crystallizations of doing framed by technique explains the determining role played by katas in the development of Japan at the beginning of the modern era and, in a different form, even today.

During the Meiji period, those who threw the weight and form of their life kata into Japan's transformative social mix played a determining role, because the force of their example amplified and reverberated through the beginning process of modernization. At the beginning of the Meiji era, the new administration, established in 1868, simultaneously had to defend itself against attempts at colonial penetration, pacify a country that had just undergone a period of unrest, and create an economic and technical foundation for its society so that industry could gain a foothold. And it succeeded. As a result of this policy, for example, the Japanese, who were familiar only with sail-power navigation, studied Western technology, and in twenty years, they built a military fleet capable of defeating the Russians, whose navy was considered one of the best at that time.

At the end of the Edo period and during the Meiji period, the warriors demonstrated an extraordinary concentration of their strength—a very real concentration. They were educated to plunge themselves completely into a specific framework. The connection to taking action characteristic of the warrior class that kata developed was within a climate of social change.

At the beginning of the Meiji era, former social structures broke down. Three factors allowed the system of identification to be transferred and expanded: the existence of a shared goal for the country—that is, moving Japan to the level of a world power; the replacement of the shogun with the emperor; and the replacement of the feudal fiefdoms with the Japanese state.

The activity of the warriors, formerly turned back within itself in the practice of martial arts, was now set to work in the transformation of a world.

To what extent can we continue to speak of kata? First of all, for the descendents of warriors, the connection to action remained the one in which they were educated through kata: dedication, concentration, and a life path that moved through a series of identifications. Yet the transformation of Japan's social and economic reality, with its inertia, broke down the specific influence of the kata and the milestones of its progression. Social models then appeared that, though originating in the kata, were animated with a new dynamic.

Certain biographies of this period bear witness to the presence of characteristics of life kata applied to the accomplishment of new objectives.[4]

In order to better delimit the notion of kata, we must enumerate the specific traits that characterize the life kata within these new social models.

First of all, a life kata means settling on a task and pouring our life into it with such intensity that life is consumed by it. Such was the case of the Akiyama brothers—Yoshifuru and Saneyuki—sons of impoverished warriors who put together the new Japanese army. After his studies in France, Yoshifuru established the Japanese cavalry while he made plans for a later confrontation with Russia. After having studied in the United States, Saneyuki became an officer in the central command of the Japanese admiralty, where he also prepared for war with Russia. The tale of their lives, entirely molded by the future of Japan, makes mention of their extreme poverty, their great asceticism, and an astonishing drive in studying new and foreign languages and technologies.

They became more and more identified with the state in its struggle with Russia, and, despising comfort and luxury, they devoted all their time to war preparations. Yoshifuru, who led the Japanese cavalry, remained faithful to a principle that he had set himself: "In the whole of life, if we achieve one single thing, life is fulfilled to perfection." Saneyuki played an essential role in the victory over the Russian fleet. He poured all of his intelligence and physical strength into the battle with Russia—clear evidence of an exceptional level of activity and an exceptional sense of strategy. After the victory, because his task and his life were accomplished, he quietly passed away.

There were numerous lives like those of the Akiyama brothers, and all of them reflected an identical model: placing themselves in the current of history that carried Japan forward, and then becoming identified, little by little, with the Japanese state by choosing a well-defined objective as a real mission for their life.

Second, the connection to the task that these individuals set for themselves passes through the persona of the double. They were vitally engaged in the service of the emperor and the country, and the obstacles they encountered were such that they were able to build the complex persona of an interiorized master-adversary. Thus Russia, in these examples, is the actual persona of an enemy, but it is also a Western country that is a source of knowledge.

Third, the preeminence of the link to the double creates a limitation, therefore a resistance vis-à-vis other social elements, and the individual begins to adopt an exclusive attitude, which is then limiting. This closed world, which forms without the support of the technical katas, is determined by the quality and complexity of the persona of the double. If this persona is sufficiently extensive, it will become diversified within certain boundaries.

Finally, the relationship between the double and the individual is sustained by the weight of the life—that is, by an identification that can extend all the way to death. Within the intensity of this relationship, death brings a balance.

Once formed, the katas are characterized by their heaviness and their rigidity. In contrast to their effectiveness at the beginning of the Meiji era, subsequently—up to the end of World War II—they played the role either of a brake or of a persistence in relation to the current initiative.

The inflexibility of Japanese military strategy in the course of World War II is due to the imposed kata structure of the most active forces of the army. The strategy that had led to victory over Russia became adopted as a model, in the form of a kata, and it continued to be pursued—but it led to catastrophe, because it was out of step with the world context, and no critical examination of any kind was socially acceptable. Katas are quite resistant to a progressive, ongoing evolution, and they can be transformed only through breaking them.

The Sino-Japanese War and especially the Russo-Japanese War were decisive experiences for Japan, and they stimulated an enthusiastic participation of the whole population. Alongside the destiny of the country, each person put his own fate at stake. The material investment was huge: the armed forces budget exceeded 48 percent of the gross national product for the years 1897–1904 (the war with Russia) and reached 55 percent between 1898 and 1900.

The military leaders of these conflicts received their education within the warrior class. Following their initiative, the newly created Japanese army was modeled on the French and German armies.

Subsequently, the victory over Russia took on mythical proportions. The organizational structure and the hierarchical system of the army took on the authority of a model that almost could not be challenged.

Victory reinforced the militaristic tendency and the respect for the army within the population. This meant that up until World War II, the correct response to the question, "What are you going to do when you grow up?" was "I'm going to be a general!"

The more Japan intensified its imperialism, the more militarism grew and the more military structures tended to rigidify. It could be said that at the beginning of World War II, the Japanese army had ferreted away real military katas and drew the strength of their dynamism through identification with the victorious army of the Meiji era.

The victory over Russia raised the status of several military figures to the designation of *gun shin* (literally, "warrior god"; *shin* is a synonym for *kami*). Following the example of the system that had formed and transformed them, the protagonists of that era became identification models for the military men of following generations who, as they faced a potential enemy, had to uphold the same relationship of superiority as had their models.

The circle of identifications was brought to completion in the central figure of the emperor—the veritable incarnation of Japan—who was considered a god and who occupied center stage in the nationalism that grew out of the Meiji era. The loyalty and devotion that had formerly been paid to the feudal lords was now carried over to the emperor.

In this way, the Japanese military built a true kata—that is, a closed world in which the search for effectiveness was unchangeable. By contrast, the other national armies evolved. At the beginning of the Meiji era, the Japanese army was at the forefront of industrial development, but, though Japan as a capitalist nation developed in conjunction with the capitalist world, the army was frozen in kata and kept itself in isolation from real or potential enemies. Rigid attachment to the model blocked the evolution of forms of strategy and training. For example, in 1940, soldiers' rifles dated from the Russo-Japanese War (1904).

This increasing rigidity became part of the totalitarian framework that dominated the country at the time. The contrast between the very great adaptability of the Meiji-era Japanese military and the inflexibility and irrational nature of the army during World War II presents a real problem. A contemporary author has commented, "I wonder if it is even the same race, the same people who built these two armies."

An analysis from the point of view of katas can provide us with answers. During World War II, the kata of the Japanese military became the dominant social model, and the populace was immediately compelled to adhere to it. Certainly, there were a good number of opposition movements, but because they were too weak, they did not resonate with the population.

Every activity then operated as much from the material as from the psychological point of view, in step with the image of the army, and the entire population was subjected to enormous pressure to become completely engaged in the war effort. When a soldier was killed in action, neighbors had to say to the parents, "Congratulations." Further, the parents, hiding their suffering, had to respond, "He was happy to die for the emperor's country."

Propaganda as well as the withholding or the distortion of information were systematically controlled and aimed to bring the population into precise alignment with the army. Thus, an atmosphere and a state of tension were created that anticipated and sanctioned any event or any conduct that related to the national objective. For example, speech was strictly controlled. All English words were forbidden and were replaced with translations into Japanese. These original words, however, were important, because they designated articles and know-how that had been brought into the country from the time of the Meiji period.

The word *emperor* assumed an extremely strong meaning. No one could speak of the emperor in an off-hand way, and when anyone spoke this word, he or she had to stand up, with a ramrod back and hands along the side of the body—at least in public places, that is, where others could see the speaker. The force that gave the kata its structure moved toward a deification of the word and the image of the emperor, and the void created by what was forbidden was insidiously filled with the development of an imperial symbolism.

So we see how all the stress brought on by the war, leading to devastation and to the most extreme kind of efforts, found its meaning and rationale in this central figure that was reinforced. We can say, therefore, that the Japanese were hurled into a kata—in the sense of life kata—that strove to find an effectiveness as conceived by the Japanese military but which was out of touch with world forces.

COLLECTIVE SUICIDES: THE BIRTH OF A KATA

At the end of World War II, numerous collective suicides took place in Japan. The most striking was the entire population of the village on Tokashiki, a small island in the Okinawa archipelago, where about four hundred people committed suicide together.

Five months before the end of the war, the island of Okinawa was surrounded by the American fleet. A few regiments of the Japanese army remained on the island with orders to fight till the death. Among them, many sailors tried to hurl themselves against the warships, using light watercraft armed with two bombs, but this strategy failed. One segment, based at Tokashiki, waited for the American landing before beginning fighting.

After intense bombardment, rumors spread through the population. According to one such rumor, the death of all civilians had been ordered so that the military could fight unhindered. According to a document published after the war, some families gathered around a grenade, which they set off; others beat each other with sticks, spades, or swords, or they cut their arteries, and so forth. In 1977, in *Background of a Myth,* Sono Ayako gives an account of the scrupulous ten years' of research she had conducted on this incident. According to her in-depth study, taking into account the difficulties in transmission, the meteorological conditions, and the incessant bombardment, no one that day was in any condition to give an order for collective suicide.

Among other accounts collected from the few survivors, Sono

Ayako particularly mentions the case of Kinjo, a boy of sixteen at the time of these events. Kinjo and his older brother killed their mother and their younger brothers and sisters, but Kinjo himself survived his own attempt at suicide. He was arrested when he tried to go to his death by attacking the American soldiers. Later, he was able to find the necessary strength to continue living only by entering the Catholic religion; he became a monk.

> The suicide order was given, and each family began to commit suicide using the few grenades we had been given. But only some of the grenades exploded, so very few families died this way.
>
> This fact caused a great deal of heartache. . . .
>
> A man grabbed a piece of wood and began to kill his wife and children. A fever of mind began to spread. We too began to kill. Some people beat their wives and children with sticks or rocks and others with sickles or knives, cutting their arteries. Others strangled them with cords. All the means that people could think of were used. The order for death had been given.
>
> No one was so inhuman as to commit suicide while leaving behind the weak, elderly, women, or children. Fathers and young boys killed their families with their own hands, and then they took their own lives after making sure that the others had really died. . . .
>
> A boy of sixteen whose body and soul had been inculcated with the education of death through the imperial, military ideology, believed that helping others to die was, without any possible doubt, the only imaginable recourse. . . .
>
> Why have I myself survived? This fact is important even from the point of view of the psychology of collective suicide. What brought about my survival was a boy's suggestion to attack the American soldiers. "We're going to die anyway, so it would be best to die in killing one more of the enemy. . . ." We decided to attack so that we would be massacred.
>
> What we thought about as we awoke from the nightmare of the

collective suicide is that perhaps someone from the family had survived. But the abnormality of the collective suicide was not that kind.

I could not harbor the slightest hope that there would be a single survivor.[5]

Sono Ayako reports the accounts of other people who, like Kinjo, escaped death unwittingly, as well as accounts of surviving Japanese soldiers—so many contradictory accounts, all devoid of any clarity except for the fact of the death by suicide of about four hundred people.

The notions of kata and of kuki, it would seem, may be able to shed light on an event of this kind. As Sono Ayako explains, it was very important, especially in the countryside, to do things together. Blame directed at anyone who acted in a different way may have been implicit, but was no less strong as a result. In the social context of the times, certain groups that were very cohesive had adopted the dominant kata of Japanese militarism much more intensely. Each person was prepared to die, and children at school learned that "a Japanese must not be captured alive."

In the compressed timescale of the group, the collective suicide on Tokashiki encompasses the mental structure of the kata—a distillation of the kata of Japanese militarism. The inhabitants killed themselves in the framework of an identification. They had been promised to death—future victims of the Americans—and each one took upon himself the imminent death of all members of the group. Their deed anticipated the death, which had to come, but they effected a substitution that moved within a framework impregnated by militaristic ideology that was located in the eyes of the others, in how they were seen by the others.

In the chronology of the facts, the idea of taking refuge in a place thought to be more secure begins to be transmitted as an order. In its rigor and intransigence, the order connects to the military system. The words then become a basis for an act in group space, reactivating the non-said, which forms the air of the group. Then the coming together takes place amid the chaos of the bombardment.

Next, the Japanese soldiers, in their role of defense, do not intervene, for their mission is to fight as long as possible, in fact until they die; it is not to protect the population. The army's aloofness is possibly seen as abandonment, and, in this extreme situation, is taken as a death order.

The unanimity of the reaction and the transition to the deed itself is problematic. The notion of kuki applied to a group whose cohesiveness is so extreme helps us to understand the beginning of this process. The movement taken by the inhabitants comes together as a kata aimed at effectiveness and dignity in death, and provides an escape from the shame and horror of being killed by the enemy.

Committing suicide is also a kind of pride, and for the inhabitants who came together in this location, giving the word is like a catalyst toward death, making it easier and also eliminating any chance of escape. The first suicide confirms reality and makes an exception impossible, because the group is bound together in this critical situation. The first death is really the death of every inhabitant.

The Tokashiki suicides took place like a kata of collective seppuku, concentrated in a brief, high-tension moment. It is only when the kata of suicide was left behind—or as Kinjo was to write much later, "waking up from the nightmare"—that Kinjo was able to see things in a different light. His kata disintegrated when he met the soldiers, and when he met other survivors who, like him, ought to have been dead.

13

KATAS TODAY

COLLAPSE AND TRANSFORMATION

The kata is a closed, rigid world, and its effectiveness depends on its impervious self-sufficiency. It is not open to an ongoing transformation. When a kata loses its effectiveness, through a separation from the context in which it operates, the whole system crumbles and the change has to be radical.

The end of World War II is an illustration of the tumbling down of katas—but also, something of the old order has remained. An example of the most striking collapse of the katas and of radical change is that of the many Japanese who, as the war was ending, were prepared to die fighting with bamboo weapons—and yet, these same people very soon after the beginning of the occupation, welcomed the Americans and passionately adopted their culture.

Ruth Benedict reports on a fact that was repeated again and again: once Japanese soldiers had been taken prisoner, following a period of complete refusal, suddenly these men would make an about-face and, with astonishing submissiveness, would move to the American side and unhesitatingly provide information on Japanese military secrets.[1]

From the point of view of Western ideas and values, this radical change appears illogical and immoral—or perhaps even incomprehensible.

Yet this kind of behavior is comparable to that of the warriors in the transition period between the old Japan and the Meiji era. All those who played an important role in opening Japan and setting up the new system had first of all strongly advocated a policy of immediate warfare against the Westerners, pitting swords against cannons. Eventually, understanding how unequal the forces were, they adopted with the same determination a strategy that represented a complete redirection of their methods, thereby turning against the tenets of traditionalism.

In fact, such an abrupt change is due to the transition from one kata to another. Even if this attitude seems to be a complete departure, this is why the relationship to what is done is not changed. Radical change through the breaking down of one kata and the rebuilding of another can be accomplished only if the cohesiveness of the groups is strong and if, in the collective psychology, there persists the idea that perfection and completeness are accessible. This connects more or less explicitly to a polytheistic conception of the world.

In this situation, when a social current assumes a unique and concentrated aspect—for example, during a crisis—the unification of various acts becomes facilitated through the mediation of katas.

SOCIAL MODELS BASED ON KATAS

With the development of capitalism, the gap widened between the katas and the way industrial production was organized. Capitalist production has no quantitative need for individuals who surpass themselves in their job through excessive dedication to the kata. It does, however, require social models that insure the cooperativeness and reliability of its workers, something that Japanese society was in the best position to provide.

In the 1980s, Japanese students and salaried workers had very uniform behavioral models—so much so that in everyday language we speak of the kata of the banker, the civil servant, the student, and so on, even though at the present time this term tends to be replaced by the word *type,* which has been borrowed from American concepts.

These models are not really katas in the sense defined in this book. Instead, these are social models, which demonstrate well-established collective conduct, but traces of the old katas can still be found in them. We see, for example, that almost all students, both boys and girls, up to the end of high school wear a dark uniform the cut of which, inspired by military uniforms, requires care in its maintenance. Also, in many high schools, hairstyles have been regulated for a long time. If such a constraint is well accepted, it is because it resides in an extension of the old katas. We need only remember the strictness of movement and attire imposed on the sons of the ancient warriors.

Similarly, the way salaried Japanese workers dress, although it is not institutionalized, is quite uniform, with each person responding to an implicit standard that he has arrived at based on how others view him.

There are many Japanese who are more or less consciously looking for a substitute for a life kata. In large, industrial Japanese corporations, we encounter "gods of the machine."* A god of the machine is a worker who has extensive experience in mechanics and thinks only about his machine, day and night, in order to perfect it.

For example, a large tire manufacturer imported several of the latest machines from the United States in order to equip his factories. Most of these machines had a god of the machine, who studied the new machine so thoroughly that he was able to improve its performance. Individuals who have this kind of exclusive connection to the machine play a dynamic role in these companies.

In a steel manufacturing company, we might encounter a god of the smelting furnace, who manages to resolve problems in the mixture and in the heat by studying the color of the flames. Companies that are now known worldwide grew out of microstructures and had such

---

Kikai no kami sama: literally, *kikai no* (of the machine,) *kami* (god,) and *sama,* a term of respectful address.

technology gods. Those who had this kind of exclusive rapport with machines played a decisive role in these companies.

The Japanese capitalist system is therefore limited not only to the production strength of the work force; it is also based on a particular relationship to technology and to taking action. The system is designed to mold and intensify the bonds that connect the work force, technical know-how, and the enterprise. The history of the Honda factory is a good example. At the beginning, the company was like one big family. The commitment to technical progress grew up around a boss-technician who was himself a god of the machine, and the commitment of the technicians was patterned exactly on this boss-master. This leader's role is no longer just a matter of managing a work force, but of husbanding a relationship to technique that grows in a favorable environment.

The position and distance of a kata in relation to the various levels of social reality vary according to the degree of its effectiveness. If it turns out to be ineffective, the kata's survival is immediately threatened, because it is too rigid to transform and adapt to new goals.

In the Edo period, katas played a fundamental role in social processes. Their importance subsequently decreased, but in different ways depending on the times, the environment, and the particular area affected. During World War II, collective behavior was registered in a kata that was located to some extent on the surface of social life. Coming out of the war, this kata was broken, and it has not been replaced by any similarly coherent structure. Yet the structure of the kata is still present, buried in the depths of the collective psyche and continuing to serve as a framework for collective behavior, such as the famous Japanese conformism, without which we would be hard-pressed to understand Japanese society's stability and steady bearing. Even in today's Japan, there are many social groups within which there persists a tendency toward structuring around a kata. Such katas are partial compared to the kata of a whole class or order.

THE PERSISTENCE OF
KATAS IN ART

The intensity that a kata can assume varies in proportion to its effectiveness in society. This is one of the reasons that katas are maintained only in a very explicit way in the realm of traditional arts, and even then, only if that art form has retained its original purity.

When efforts are made to try to integrate new elements, for example in *ikebana* (the art of flower arrangement), the kata disappears, because this mixing is only a beginning or a trial that cannot form a kata, because it has not achieved its perfection. The trial may remain at the level of curiosity or of something pretty, or with time it can set in motion a new form of kata unless too many elements are brought into play. Most often, such efforts lead to dispersion rather than to inherent crystallization into a kata.

The situation is the same with calligraphy or painting, which, up to a certain point, can tolerate a renewal of motifs. Attempts to add new elements from the Western world (for example, letters of the European alphabet) fall outside the limiting framework of the kata. It turns into something else, and the result is unable to achieve an impact of the same intensity as that of the original katas.

In order to illustrate the coherence of the kata, we can draw on the example of an experienced Japanese painter who, having learned and worked with oil painting in Paris, found it very difficult, if not impossible, to produce a satisfactory result when he applied this technique in Japan. In fact, for him, his technical skill was delineated within a coherent whole, and his perception of Japanese reality was filtered through the traditional representation mode. He could swing back and forth from one mode to the other, from one universe to the other, but the adaptation resulted in failure. Synthesis is possible, but only through breaking the kata.

The changes that come about in the course of the transmission of katas in karate clarify the internal transformation limits that the katas support, because, unlike in the previous examples, this transformation is most often involuntary. The full meaning of a series of moves can be grasped only when there is a correct gauge of the presence of the double, the multiform adversary. In fact, contrary to what we might think, the move as such is very difficult to transmit.

At a level that is not very advanced, the spoken explanation is often limited to indicating the position of the adversary, without commenting on the transmitted techniques themselves. At certain moments, this information is very valuable for someone who dives into the kata through an effort of introspection. Within the same kata, we sometimes find both the attack and the counterattack. This means that the ongoing series of moves of the kata includes at any moment what the virtual adversary has done or will do.

In our time, however, the presence of the adversary has become very fuzzy in the imagination of the *karatekas*,* because real combat is rare and training combat is often limited to competitions that are regulated by certain rules. By obeying these rules, the imaginary adversary becomes very light and less cunning.

This is why the execution of the kata, even when it is empty, becomes more spectacular and there is no longer any questioning of the meaning of the moves. This is the basis for the criticism: "This kind of kata is only a karate flower." It is nice to look at but it has no substance. If the adversary is everywhere and is sly, every move reflects the attack, and the execution of the kata, untouched by the look of those watching, becomes less spectacular. When the adversary eases off, the tension lets go, giving rise to an engagement in moves that are more like bodily gestures. Tension moves out from our interior space and is visible to the eyes of the onlookers. In real combat, the look from others is set aside; all that matters is the person we are facing.

The transmission of *kata,* in the real meaning of this term, takes

---

Karateka, a word that refers to a practitioner of karate, is a Japanese word that is also used in Western karate dōjōs.

place alongside the prevailing sportsmanlike tendency, and actually happens when the practice tends toward a form of gyō, in which the adversary appears as a persona of death. This explains the ever-widening gap between what is transmitted to the majority through the prevailing current and that which, in spite of appearances, is to be found on the periphery. When the adversary disappears completely, the execution of the kata becomes a simple sequence of moves, and the kata is then understood as a gymnastic exercise that includes a few moves connected to combat or as a psychotherapeutic procedure. With that, it is inevitable that the practitioner becomes disconnected from the kata, all the more because the spectacle brings in a third person as observer.

THE KATA AND THE STRUCTURE
OF SMALL GROUPS

In studying the psychological structure of the kata, we can identify two traits within the dominant model of small groups in Japan: the existence of a shared center of identification, and a certain type of resistance in relation to the outside. The type of social group that is dominant and is to be found at all levels of Japanese society is that described by Chie Nakane in *Japanese Society*.[2]

In this type of group there is always the representation of a way of being—not an ideal one (we are not speaking here of a kata), and yet a desirable way of being to which members of the group are striving. The way this takes place is close to that of a kata, because this image occupies a central position and involves a multifaceted persona in which, notably, the representation of an entire hierarchy is concentrated. The chief of the group, placed at the top of the pyramid, is, just because of the position he holds, bound to certain identification with this collective image.

His position is justified by the appreciation of others, and his power, which is more apparent than real, consists mainly of formulating the decisions that are expected by the group as a whole. The principal quality of a chief is to be sufficiently sensitive to the expression and the air of the group in order to be able to see where the group is headed. In Japan, no matter what type of group it is (home, business, state), everyone insists on the importance of *wa*. This term includes two ideas: "nice agreement, intimacy, calm, balance" and "assemble, add together." Written with a different ideogram, it means "circle." The quality chief implements the *wa* within the group by modulating whatever would bring harshness into the relationships or severity into the opinions.

This type of functioning is effective only in groups of limited size, even if a very hierarchical structure is present. A group with larger numbers of members will informally divide up into a chain of smaller groups. The head of a small group, then, still has a place—one both within the hierarchy and in relation to the members of his own group.

Because the group is partially based on identification, exchanges with the outside are limited. In Japanese groups, the distinction between what is inside and outside the group is quite pronounced. This can be seen in the frequent use of the expression *uchi no* (*no*, "of, belonging to"; *uchi*, "home," "my place," "inside") to designate belonging to a group. This is the commonest way of referring to a spouse (*uchi no niobo, uchi no hito,* sometimes shortened to just *uchi*). The same expression also designates belonging to a company (*uchi no kaisha*), regardless of an individual's function—in a university for example, or through a connection with the president of a company (*uchi no shachio*) or with a chief (*uchi no kachio*). The same term is used to designate the relationship to the group or a relationship to a person.

Identification with the group is characterized by the well-known fact that a Japanese person will introduce himself not by saying his name and then "professor" or his name and then whatever his position is, but instead by saying his name, then "from University X" or his name and "from Company Y."

KATA AND KARATE

The karate that has been practiced for a long time in the island of Okinawa did not spread to the rest of the country and did not become part of the ensemble of traditional martial arts until recent times.

The Japanese public usually places karate at the bottom of the hierarchy of martial arts after swordsmanship, archery, aikido, and judo. Compared to the followers of other martial arts, the social status and the study level of karate amateurs are very often inferior. Yet the internal organization of clubs and groups does not vary a great deal from one martial art to another. In this respect, karate can be considered representative of the whole field of martial arts.

There are many schools and styles in karate, and tension between schools is prevalent. Each style tends to close itself off in its own world, convinced that it alone has the truth, like a microcosm segmented into grades at the top of which reigns a master, representing absolute attainment. The more an individual trains, the more integrated into this world he becomes. He must place himself completely outside these closed worlds in order to be able to recognize the existence of other schools with comparable structures and levels.

The styles and their names appeared in karate in the twentieth century. In Okinawa, the style is that of a master, and it did not get transmitted as such. For example, although certain variants of katas bear his name, the great master Matsumura Sōkon (1808–1895) did not leave behind a style or a school. Individuals simply referred to the *te* (karate) of Matsumura. Moreover, at this time training took place from night until dawn in out-of-the-way places (in the woods, on a beach, and so forth) with very few disciples.

The names of the styles and the schools appeared in the 1930s, when karate spread throughout Japan and its teaching began to settle into a fixed place—the dōjō—in which the practice returned to the teaching system of the traditional budō. Later on, the system of grades was borrowed from judo. The number of students gradually increased, and karate began to be very widely disseminated. The bases of different styles appeared with this institutional development of karate and with the advent of the professional karateka.

Before this, the teaching of karate was not a professional activity. Masters of the classical period practiced their craft and had no need of disciples to support them, so they could demand a great deal of their disciples. The master had only to choose a successor from among his disciples, who were always very limited in number. The teaching then was very personal and could vary a great deal depending on the quality and character of each disciple. With this esoteric character, karate remained relatively unknown for a long time.

The founding masters of the classical styles known today came out of this former teaching system that is at the origin of karate. These masters played an important role in its development on the level both of technique and of concepts. For the first generation of students who discovered karate, the relationship with the master was personal, close in nature to the former system, and many of them would visit other masters.

With the institutionalization of the teaching, the students at the dōjō became numerous, the relationship with the master became less personal and took place through the group, which then tended to become exclusive. In fact, the more the students became connected to a practice, the more imposing the persona of the master became. In their eyes, their master became the greatest master, which prevented them from seeing that a different one might also be good, or even better.

We can take Shotokan style as an example of how a style was formed. Master Funakoshi set himself up in Tokyo in 1921, at the age of fifty-four. According to Otsuka, founder of the Wado-ryū style and one of Funakoshi's first disciples, when he first visited his master, Funakoshi was working as a desk clerk in a boardinghouse and was living in a fifty-square-foot room. In the evening, he gave karate training in the main room of this boarding house. These were the conditions in which he began to spread karate throughout Japan's main island, as other teachers were doing the same thing. Master Funakoshi died in 1957 at the age of ninety, having achieved great fame in karate circles and leaving behind many disciples, each one claiming he was transmitting the master's true teaching and claiming also that he knew the secret or the heart of karate.

Today, there are numerous competing streams within this one Shotokan style, and each one claims to be the true Shotokan.

Master Funakoshi's teaching continued to increase in importance from 1921 to 1940, but during the war, he gradually stopped, as did all cultural activity in Japan. Nevertheless, during the conflict, the teaching of karate was maintained in several universities by Master Funakoshi's disciples, who had been trained before the war and who, for the most part, had other jobs. This strategy meant a continuation of the rigorous education that demanded so much work from the students and within which a friendly style of training held an important place. Yet the context was in the process of changing, and a sports-oriented practice was on the rise.

After the war, Master Funakoshi was eighty years old and had greatly reduced the amount of time he was teaching. Yet the karatekas who began at this time stressed the importance of their connection with him and used that to prove the authenticity of their school. It is the same in other styles and in other martial arts. In aikido, for example, many masters stress their qualities as disciples of master Ueshiba, the founder of this art. We might well wonder about this need to affirm the authenticity of a style by justifying a direct descent from the founder. Why is there this necessity to acquire legitimacy by claiming to be the direct student of such and such a master?

Let's now look at the group practices of the karate club at the University of Tokyo, where I studied and where I trained assiduously from 1967 to 1971. The training is difficult and is done daily, and each person implicitly commits to working at it for a long time. The teaching is fundamentally a transmission from student to student, following a hierarchy modeled on university promotions. It takes place mainly through the repetition of technical moves and katas. A single move is often repeated a few thousand times in succession.

Training takes place in the university dōjō. Students look after its upkeep themselves. Before and after each training session, the first- and second-year students who occupy the lower part of the hierarchy clean the dōjō.

The learning cycle has progressive stages based on repeating what higher-level students are doing. The individual who is learning teaches beginners to do what he is doing. The professor makes corrections and provides general instruction, but transmission takes place from one generation to the next.

Daily training is rounded out with five or six more intensive training periods per year. During these sessions, each about one week in duration, which take place in the mountains or at the sea, the whole group lives together, and each person pushes himself to the limit in about six hours a day of training.

The group is closely knit but at the same time very hierarchically structured. Social relationships in the group are formalized by the use of bowing and by the ritual of the training sessions themselves. The form of address used is "Oss," which is an abbreviated form of military salutation used in martial arts groups, by sportsmen, and by thieves. A lower-level student bows when he uses this form of address, and the student from the level above him repeats it, remaining erect or giving a slight nod of the head.

Each training session begins and ends with a bow, followed by a brief moment of meditation in a kneeling position; the practitioners sit on the heels. Before and after each combat engagement, each student also bows to his opponent. The hierarchy functions through successive links. For example, a student from the first or second year will respect a fourth-year student, but the more advanced student's relationship with the less advanced student will be distant. The group's cohesion works through the links in the chain.

Students of first and second year must be obedient. In certain universities, the work expected of them is a kind of servitude and is accompanied by bullying that can descend into torture. If the relationship of submission is evident, the dependency is balanced by the older ones taking things in hand. The higher-level student will invite the younger ones to a restaurant, pay for the meal, and eventually introduce them to girls.

Students from the final year are regarded as representing the right way to behave, and they serve as models of identification. In this system, the respect that is owed toward those one level above takes precedence over the respect due in Japan to a person who is older, even if only one year older. This relationship is characterized by the form of address, with respect moving in one direction, and with condescension that can go so far as scorn moving in the other. The head acts as if he were above all levels.

The captain of the club is the head of the fourth-year team and is chosen for his good qualities that are recognized by everyone. Group harmony depends on him. He is the entry point that leads to a larger circle of identification. He represents those by whom he has been trained. At the same time, the beginners know very well that four years before, he was in the same place where they are now. Those who trained him belong to earlier generations, and certain ones among them return sometimes to the dōjō and support the training. Their presence stands for that of a master who is supposed to be better and stronger.

In this martial art environment, an individual can play the role of master even if he does not really have the quality, to the extent that he is in relationship to a stronger image. It could be a living person that he identifies with (but who stays in the background) or a person from the recent past whose line he is continuing.

Along these lines, the photo of Master Funakoshi is to be found in many karate studios belonging to associations that are more or less antagonistic to each other but all of whom are bolstering their authenticity with this lineage. Each one of them is a closed world. The structure of the kata is held in place in each one to the extent that the series of identifications is made in relation to an image of perfection. The image is that of a mythical personage whose outlines have been blurred, either by the media, if the person is still alive, or, if the person has passed, by making a legend of him.

I experienced this myth myself. After university, I followed the teaching of a master for three years, systematically rejecting the authority of all others. As long as I remained within the group, admitting that others were as good as us was impossible for me. The existence of this closed, self-contained world and the persona of the master allowed me to galvanize my energy in the training and to make progress in technique. The master was an adversary who was effective but also who dwelled within me. In this closed world, the persona of the master-adversary was simple because it was directed only toward one person.

In leaving him, I realized that this master was only one of many masters. The persona that came down hard on me and, at the same time, that I strove toward had moved into the distance as it multiplied. I could objectively observe other groups, and I could discover qualities in them that were missing in my old group and that represented complementary elements. It then seemed to me that each of the groups or styles were bearers of a tradition in the katas that they transmitted, and taken together, they constituted the various facets of a discipline. From then on, the new persona of the master-adversary included for me the multiplicity of these groups, which, through their katas, took me back to the past.

In the organization of karate, the hermetically sealed nature of the groups is one of the constituent elements of the desired effectiveness. In fact, in the dominant structure of small groups, the circle of identification goes hand in hand with the creation of an inner world and therefore of a resistance in relation to what is outside. The effectiveness of the group leads to a confrontation and then to a meeting with groups of the same type—that is, toward a permeability and an opening to the outside.

The central persona of the master-adversary that we developed in relation to martial arts allows us to see, from this angle, that the external world is reintegrated into the circle of identification and tends to enrich it.

When effectiveness is no longer delineated, except by standards that are internal to the group, and those standards then become partial—which tends to be the case for the majority of martial arts, because society no longer offers unregulated fighting grounds—the groups close themselves off from one another, and each one claims to be more effective than the others.*

The form of the kata is effective in moving forward in a chosen direction—in art or in work—because it allows the expenditure of a great deal of effort. The scope and the richness of the persona of the double determine the level of effectiveness that will be attained.

Even when we adhere to a myth, it is possible to devote ourselves completely, but the persona of the double, in becoming mythical, shrinks and turns into a simple logic. The effectiveness that is sought inside a group of this kind is subject to the limitations of this logic. In the rigid and very hierarchical form of group that we have described, the simplification of the persona of identification harbors the danger of a susceptibility to various kinds of fascism.

Relations within the group presume effective connections that support the group's cohesiveness. The reciprocal relationship of taking charge and dependency between superiors and inferiors provides us with a key to some of these relations. In the same way, in a corporation, the superior takes charge of subordinates and the subordinate can let go in dependency. We can also compare this attitude with that of the chief—one of his qualities is to know how to be carried by the group. A current Japanese expression is, "Let's do that by carrying Mr. X on our

---

*In judo, on the other hand, there is a consensus on a well-defined form of effectiveness determined by its rules as a sport, but in the realm of martial arts, judo is often considered a game or sport—one that that came from *jiu-jitsu*—and not as a martial art in the true sense of the word (budō).

shoulders," and Mr. X designates the person playing the role of chief in his capacity of assuring the unity of the group, even though his effectiveness in the matter may be negligible.

Certain Japanese authors call this type of attitude *passive love*. These relations develop on a field prepared by dependent, passive love (amae), which—as we have seen—unites the child and his mother in a reciprocal relationship. In this relationship, the identification of one person with another generally takes precedence over an affirmation of anyone's separateness, and it is on this basis that the communication of the non-said is developed in society.

The effective relations between people on the same level are influenced in a general way by this model. One of them will tend, either momentarily or in an ongoing way, to assume the role of the elder. Every person has an experience of one or the other of these positions.

CONCLUSION

As we come to the end of an analysis that shows that kata is indeed a complicated notion—and if, in spite of all that, we were to define *kata* in a few words, we might say that it is a structure of the act and of the relation to the double (in the broadest sense of the term—someone else or something else) that is recorded in a stable, hierarchical social system.

The kata covers both a practice and a social conception of life. Because it simultaneously extends to technical, psychological, and social realms, which have a tendency to blend together, it is difficult to force the kata into the usual categories of analysis.

In analyzing the notion of *kata,* I have been drawn to using the term in a sense that is unusual in Japanese. Rather than the kata of the warriors or the kata of art or the life kata, in Japanese we would speak of "way" (dō). Yet in order to avoid having this notion include anything subjective or metaphysical, I choose the word *kata,* because, in its usual meaning, it covers a reality that is easy to delimit, and the extended meaning that I have given it remains precise.

Several factors allow the structure of the kata to be defined:

- The kata is an act that aims at effectiveness. The practice of the kata is done through the repetition of codified, technical moves. The repetition aims at a perfect execution of the act, and is to be found in a movement toward perfection. This practice is based on a conception of technique that can be summed up as: "Technique and the man are one." Striving toward an ideal model engenders rigidity, and at the same time, it sets energy in motion. The kata is a privileged means of maintaining and transmitting a tradition.

- The mobilization of the energy in the kata takes place through a process of interiorization and identification. The image of perfection becomes concrete through identification with what we have called the multiple personae of the double. The mobilization of the energy and the commitment required by the kata presume an exchange with a social milieu in which the kata is accepted and admired as an ideal form, at least in an implicit way. Bringing the kata into being depends on a social form of relationships to others, which support building an identification persona. These relationships must be stable and hierarchical within a strong group structure. The persona of the double integrates a complex series of identifications, termed succinctly as the persona of the master-adversary, because it is at this level that the ideal image, contradictions, and conflicts are bound together. The technical form of the kata provides a foundation that allows the balancing of this paradoxical relationship in which the energy directed at the ideal persona is turned back or reversed like a mirror, in the form of a persecution. In martial arts, technique is a technique of death, and death is present in the image of the master, who eventually is loaded with the weight of all his adversaries. The kata includes a technique for the reorganization of perception.

- Historically, the structure of the kata took shape at the heart of the warrior class during the Sakoku period, a time when Japan was closed to all foreign influence. The kata was the mode of expression and of action for this dominant class, for whom it represented their conception of life. For the warrior class, technique was combat, and effectiveness was death. During the Sakoku period—a period synonymous with closure but also with peace and social stability—combat became a martial art, and the confrontation with death became the predominant social value through a process of the individual moving within himself, which constituted the psychological structuring of the katas. The katas were developed in a stable, hierarchical society that promoted the precise delimiting of a field and composition of a series of identifications. Within this society, which was turned toward stability and continuity, the form of the kata, in taking shape and becoming established, became a privileged instrument of technical and psychological training. The structure of the kata, within which the dominant class had shaped its life, was extended to the whole of Japanese society by the end of the Sakoku period.

Today, katas are explicitly preserved only in the domain of art, but, for several centuries, warriors used the kata to create a psychological structure and a relationship to taking action that outlived the group that had given them life. In its multiple dimensions, little by little, the kata filtered into new forms of production and contributed, among other things, to shaping in a specific way the relationship of the Japanese worker to his work. It still operates in numerous segments of society, often in a diffused way. It is hard to discern, but nevertheless, it is very much present and carries the weight of a tradition that is several centuries old.

NOTES

CHAPTER 1.
TESSHU, OR A MODEL LIFE

1. Katsube Masanaga, *Bushidō. Collection of Documents on the Life of Yamaoka Tesshu* (Tokyo: Kadokawa Shotu Publishing, 1971).
2. Toshihiko Izutsu, *Le kōan zen,* in *Documents spirituels* (Paris: Fayard, 1978).

CHAPTER 2.
KATA, OR "TECHNIQUE AND THE MAN ARE ONE"

1. Watsuji Tetsuro, *Sakoku* (Tokyo: Chikuma, 1964); *Fudo* (Tokyo: Chikuma, 1963).

CHAPTER 3.
CLOSING JAPAN AND COMING BACK TO ONESELF

1. Watsuji Tetsuro, *Sakoku.*
2. Ibid.
3. J. Berque, *Espace et société au Japon. La notion de Fudo,* in *Mondes Asiatiques,* no. 16, 289–309.

4. Sigmund Freud, *Totem and Taboo*, The International Library of Psychology Series (London: Routledge, 1999), 29.

5. Ibid., 30.

6. Kozo Yamamura and Yasukichi Yasuba, eds., *Henken no kozo* (Tokyo: NHK Bukkusa, 1967).

7. Sato Tadao, *Hadaka no Nihonjin* (Tokyo: Kobunsha, 1958).

8. Ibid.

9. Ibid.

10. Ibid.

11. Ibid.

12. Ibid.

13. Kuki Shuzo, *Iki no Kozo* (Tokyo: Iwanami Shoten, 1930) Hiroshi Nara, J. Thomas Rimer, and Jon Mark Mikkelsen, trans., *Iki no Kozo*, in *The Structure of Detachment: The Aesthetic Vision of Kuki Shuzo* (Honolulu: University of Hawaii Press, 2004).

14. Ibid.

15. Ibid.

16. Ibid.

17. Ibid.

18. Ibid.

19. Ibid.

20. Ibid.

21. Ibid.

22. Ibid.

23. Ibid.

CHAPTER 4.
KAMI AND JAPANESE POLYTHEISM

1. Watanabe Shoichi, *Nihon-Shi Kara mita Nihonjin* (Tokyo: Sangyō Nōritsu Tanki Daigaku Shuooabbu, 1973).

2. Ono Susumu, *Nihongo no Nenrin* (Tokyo: Shincho-sha, 1966).

CHAPTER 5.
THE KATAS OF THE SOCIAL ORDERS
IN THE EDO PERIOD

1. See Doi Takeo, *Amae no Kozo* (Tokyo: Kobundo, 1971).

CHAPTER 7.
THE GYŌ AND SELF-INVESTMENT

1. Daisetsu Suzuki, *Zen Buddhism and Its Influence on Japanese Culture* (New York: Pantheon, 1959).
2. Kenji Tokitsu, *La voie du karaté* (Paris: Éditions du Seuil, 1979).

CHAPTER 8.
DEATH AND TIME

1. Daidoji Yuzan, *Pensée fondamentale de la voie du guerrier* (n.p., 1700). The influence of this book continued up until the end of the World War II.
2. Yamamoto Jocho, *Hagakure.*
3. *Écrits sur les cinq elements.* For a detailed analysis, see "L'état d'esprit en stratégie" in Miyamoto Musashi, *Gorin-no-shu* (Paris: DésIris, 1998), 53 and following.
4. Ibid, 55.
5. Ibid.
6. Yagyū Munemori, *Heido Kaden Sho.*
7. Takuan, *Fudochi Shimmyo roku.* This book on swordsmanship was addressed to Yagyū Munenori, but it subsequently had a great influence on all warriors. It deals with the state of mind that is required to practice swordsmanship.
8. Niwa Jurozaemon, *Tengu Gei Jutsu Ron* (n.p.,1729).
9. Michel Tournier, *Vendredi ou les limbes du Pacifique* (Paris: Éditions du Minuit, 1969).
10. Toshihiko Izutsu, *Le kôan zen* (Paris: Fayard, 1978).

CHAPTER 9.
THE PSYCHOLOGICAL
ASPECT OF KATA

1. Kenji Tokitsu, *Miyamoto Musashi* (Paris: DésIris, 1998), 31. The following quotations are from this same source.
2. This book has appeared in French as *Miyamoto Musashi*. In English it has appeared in various editions under the title *The Book of Five Rings*.
3. Minamoto Sugane (1788–1866), *Initiation to Swordsmanship*.
4. Ibid.
5. Miyamoto Musashi, *Gorin-no-shu*, "L'état d'esprit en stratégie," 25.
6. Gichin Funakoshi, *Twenty Precepts for the Way of Karate*.

CHAPTER 11.
THE WARRIOR'S KATA IN
CONTEMPORARY SOCIETY

1. Yukio Mishima, *Initiation to the Hagakure*. [Translated from the author's French translation of the original. —*Trans*.]
2. Minami Hiroshi, *The Psychology of the Japanese*, Albert R. Ikoma, trans. (Toronto: University of Toronto Press, 1972).
3. Ibid.
4. Yukio Mishima, *Initiation to the Hagakure*.
5. Minami Hiroshi, *The Psychology of the Japanese*.
6. Yukio Mishima, *Initiation to the Hagakure*.
7. *Hagakure*.
8. Minami Hiroshi, *The Psychology of the Japanese*.
9. Yukio Mishima, *Confessions of a Mask* (New York: New Directions Publishing, 1988).
10. Published in English under the title *Forbidden Colors*.
11. Yukio Mishima, *Initiation to the Hagakure*.
12. The facts related here are taken from information in the *Asahi* newspaper for November 1970 and April 1971.

CHAPTER 12.
EFFECTIVENESS AND WEIGHT
OF THE KATAS

1. Yamamoto Shichihei, *"Kuki" no kenkyu* [The Study of "Air"] (Tokyo: Bungei Shunju, 1977).
2. Ibid.
3. Ibid.
4. See several examples, laid out very precisely, in Siba Ryotaro's *Sakano ue no kumo,* a well-documented work on Meiji-era Japan (Tokyo: Bungei Shunju, 1967–1972, 6 vols).
5. Sono Ayako, *Background of a Myth* (1973).

CHAPTER 13.
KATAS TODAY

1. Ruth Benedict, *The Chrysanthemum and the Sword: Patterns of Japanese Culture* (Boston: Houghton Mifflin, 1989).
2. Chie Nakane, *Japanese Society* (Berkeley: University of California Press, 1970).

INDEX

BOOKS OF RELATED INTEREST

Aikido and Words of Power
The Sacred Sounds of Kototama
by William Gleason

The Last Lama Warrior
The Secret Martial Art of Tibet
by Yogi Tchouzar Pa

Shoninki: The Secret Teachings of the Ninja
The 17th-Century Manual on the Art of Concealment
by Master Ninja Natori Masazumi

Shaolin Qi Gong
Energy in Motion
by Shi Xinggui

Iron Shirt Chi Kung
by Mantak Chia

The Inner Structure of Tai Chi
Mastering the Classic Forms of Tai Chi Chi Kung
by Mantak Chia and Juan Li

Wisdom Chi Kung
Practices for Enlivening the Brain with Chi Energy
by Mantak Chia

The Spiritual Practices of the Ninja
Mastering the Four Gates to Freedom
by Ross Heaven

INNER TRADITIONS • BEAR & COMPANY
P.O. Box 388
Rochester, VT 05767
1-800-246-8648
www.InnerTraditions.com

Or contact your local bookseller